BR TRACTION
in colour~2

The use of Class 50s on humble departmental workings
became commonplace during the late 1980s. Carrying the
original version of Network SouthEast livery, with angled
stripes on the cabsides, No 50034 *Furious* climbs Horfield
Bank on the outskirts of Bristol with a lengthy engineers'
train on 15 June 1988.   *Michael Mensing*

PAUL SHANNON
BR TRACTION
in colour ~ 2

LONDON
IAN ALLAN LTD

Contents

First published 1989

ISBN 0 7110 1871 5

© Ian Allan Ltd 1989

Published by Ian Allan Ltd, Shepperton, Surrey; and printed by Ian Allan Printing Ltd at their works at Coombelands in Runnymede, England

Front cover:
Class 90 electric No 90008 heads north out of Carlisle with the 15.30 Euston-Glasgow on 22 June 1989. *D. McAlone*

Previous page:
The diverted 6V39 Mossend-Margam arrives at Settle Junction in the care of Nos 20075/23 on 11 March 1989. *Paul Shannon*

This page:
An unidentified Class 31/1 is seen in the Croal valley, two miles west of Bolton, with the 16.20 Manchester Victoria-Blackpool North on Saturday 6 August 1988. Paul Shannon

Introduction

In 1982 the concept of the business sector became a reality on British Rail. Responsibility for the marketing, resources and financial results of each area of operation was shifted from the five geographical regions, which broadly speaking were successors to the individual companies of pre-Nationalisation days, to the five business sectors which exist today: InterCity, Provincial, Network SouthEast, Railfreight and Parcels. In this major shake-up of railway administration the old regions were not dispensed with altogether — indeed a new Anglia Region was established in 1988, bringing the total to six — but their role would from now on be limited to the day-to-day operation and maintenance of the railway, and the implementation of policy decisions made by the different sectors.

The Sectorisation of British Rail has made its mark on day-to-day operations in a number of important respects. The most immediately obvious is the partial abandonment of the 'corporate image' policy of the 1960s, the policy which BR once regarded as crucial to successful marketing of its services and which led to the wholesale application of blue and grey or just plain blue, even down to the narrow-gauge locomotives and stock on the Vale of Rheidol Railway! Now the railways are certainly more colourful, with a proliferation of liveries for different sectors and sub-sectors, even if some of the more outlandish colour schemes have hardly met with universal approval. Less obvious but equally significant have been the changes in the deployment of BR traction and rolling stock. Gone are the days of common pools of equipment: by the late 1980s each locomotive and carriage had been allotted to a specific sector or sub-sector, which as the prime user would be responsible for meeting all its running and maintenance costs. This does not preclude the borrowing of resources from one sector to another; such borrowing may occur not only in emergencies such as locomotive failures, but also as part of the planned programme in order to achieve economies of scale on certain parts of the network. On the BR system as a whole the overriding factor in deploying traction and other resources is now the commodity being carried, rather than the region which it is being carried in. Some striking examples of this policy are found in Railfreight operations, where locomotives allocated to a particular depot may find themselves working to virtually any part of the network within a specific group of services; further details are given in the Railfreight chapter. A further way in which the business sectors are affecting what we see on BR today is in the design and specification of new rolling stock. Most locomotive types arising from the 1955 Modernisation Plan were intended to a greater or lesser degree as mixed traffic machines, of which the Class 47 is a classic example, whereas the new motive power designs of the 1980s have almost all been developed with a specific business sector in mind. There are, of course, other equally far-reaching effects of sectorisation, but these will suffice as an introduction to our look at railway operations in the late 1980s, at a time when visual interest abounds throughout the system.

The 13.44 Penzance-London Paddington InterCity 125 service approaches Burngullow on 16 February 1988, powered by cars 43019 *City of Swansea/Dinas, Abertawe* (front) and 43174 (rear). On the right is the start of the freight-only branch to Drinnick Mill and Parkandillack, whilst the derelict structure of Burngullow signalbox stands on the left. *Paul Shannon*

CHAPTER ONE

InterCity

The name 'InterCity' was first applied to BR's long-distance express trains back in 1966; the name has certainly stood the test of time and its use has even been extended to other railway administrations, notably the Deutsche Bundesbahn. In the context of BR's present-day division into business sectors, the InterCity Sector largely comprises those services which are regarded as financially viable. The last year of government subsidy for InterCity was 1987-88, and any subsequent shortfall in income versus expenditure will need to be made good from profits made by Railfreight or (less likely) Parcels. Having achieved its highest-ever real growth in earnings of 7% in 1987-88, the mood of the InterCity Sector is one of optimism, and subsidies from whatever source are not expected to remain necessary for long. In the main today's InterCity services are the same services which were marketed as such in the 1960s and 1970s, but there are some notable exceptions. These include the Glasgow-Edinburgh corridor, which was transferred in 1982 to Provincial, and the London-Weymouth line which was incorporated into Network SouthEast.

The staple motive power of the InterCity Sector is the High Speed Train, or the IC125 unit as it is now more commonly (and meaningfully) known. The first routes to receive their quota of these units were those on the Western Region, so it is appropriate to begin our look at InterCity with the current scene on that region. The gentle gradients and curves on the prime Western Region routes make them eminently suitable for the IC125 unit: trains can run at their maximum speed for almost all of the route between the outskirts of London and Chippenham (on the Bristol line) or Bristol Parkway (on the Cardiff line). Routes to both Bristol and Cardiff have witnessed an increase in patronage in recent years, and loadings are good on the approximately hourly service on each line. Many of the Bristol trains in fact start or terminate at Weston-super-Mare, and most South Wales services run to and from Swansea, also calling at the intermediate stations of Neath, Port Talbot (recently designated a 'Parkway' station) and Bridgend. Looking at the weekday train schedule for winter 1988-89, points reached further afield by IC125 units include an overnight train to and from Fishguard, two morning departures from Milford Haven with one return service in the evening, and a handful of workings extended between Weston-super-Mare and Taunton. Most of these services are achieved by using marginal time in IC125 diagrams, ie when their use on the main routes is not required. Pullman facilities are provided on one morning journey from Swansea to London and one evening journey in the reverse direction; this train caters for the growing market of long-distance

Below:
Twin Class 31 motive power was regularly provided for the Saturdays-only train from Manchester to Paignton during summer 1988, and also on some occasions for the new holiday train from Rose Grove to the same destination. On 6 August 1988 Nos 31433 and 31467 pass Cockwood Harbour with the 10.10 from Manchester, formed of the usual smart rake of InterCity-liveried stock. *David Moulden*

business travellers and is called, appropriately enough, the 'Red Dragon Pullman'. Bristol too benefits from a Pullman service which is mentioned in more detail below.

When the case was examined for extending IC125 trains to services between London and the West Country, the outcome was not a foregone conclusion. Whilst the routes to Bristol and South Wales were already suitable for high speed running, the direct route to the Southwest via the Berks & Hants line still had the characteristics of a secondary railway, with low line speeds and antiquated semaphore signalling virtually all the way from Reading (exclusive) to Penzance. Furthermore the route itself is a sinuous one, so not a lot could be done to raise line speeds by simply realigning the track.

Consideration was given to routeing all London-West Country services via Bristol, beyond which point they could share tracks with cross-country services on the northeast/southwest axis. In the event this idea was rejected, and instead the whole route from Reading to Plymouth has been progressively upgraded, with the last vestiges of mechanical signalling being abolished in 1987. Now there are line speeds reaching 110mph on parts of the Berks & Hants line, and between 90mph and 100mph on the line from Taunton to Exeter. And even though the full speed potential of the IC125 unit cannot be realised on these services, its use is justified by factors such as its superior acceleration compared with conventional locomotives and the improved comfort and facilities which it can offer to its passengers. On weekdays, again taking the winter 1988-89 timetable as an example, there are six trains each way between London and Penzance, and a further six down and five up workings between London and Plymouth.

Most of these are routed via the Berks & Hants line, and over the westernmost section beyond Plymouth they provide a local service between intermediate stations on behalf of Provincial Sector. One of the Penzance trains has been designated the 'Golden Hind Pullman' since October 1987; the up working is the first departure of the day from Penzance and provides the fastest timings between there and London, covering the 305 miles in 4hr 41min with nine intermediate stops. A second Pullman service operates to and from the West Country, but this time serving a different market. This is the 'West Country Pullman', which runs between London and Paignton. Instead of providing a morning arrival in London and an evening departure, the 'West Country Pullman' works out from London in the late morning and returns from Paignton during the afternoon; in both directions it runs via Bristol. With this particular service BR has the needs of the growing conference market in Torbay in mind.

Three further domestic IC125 services on the Western Region remain to be mentioned, all using routes 'owned' by the Provincial Sector. One operates over the Golden Valley line, serving Kemble, Stroud, Stonehouse, Gloucester and Cheltenham. Three services are provided in each

Below:
Survivors of the BR/EE Type 4 D400 locomotives, the Class 50, are now largely employed on Network SouthEast and departmental duties, since their comparatively high maintenance costs make them an unattractive proposition for top-ranking InterCity services. On 13 November 1988, however, No 50039 *Implacable* is seen piloting failed No 50032 *Courageous* on the Sundays-only 08.30 Exeter St Davids-London Paddington turn. The location is Great Cheverell, between Westbury and Pewsey on the Berks & Hants line. *Ian Gould*

direction, two of them giving a peak-hour service to and from London, and the third using marginal time from London to operate a daytime 'Cheltenham Spa Express' which actually runs as far as Great Malvern before returning to London in the afternoon. The second operates over the Cotswold line, serving Worcester and principal intermediate stations. Again three services each way are provided on weekdays, with timings arranged similarly to those on the Cheltenham route; the morning up trains and evening down trains are extended from/to Hereford. The third is the 'Stratford-upon-Avon Pullman', an out-and-back working from London which uses the IC125 set from the 'Golden Hind'. This was an innovation for summer 1988 and provided not only the first ever IC125 service to Stratford, but also the town's first direct rail link with the capital for a very long time.

The Western Region domestic IC125 fleet consists of 32 sets, divided between maintenance depots at Old Oak Common (London), St Philip's Marsh (Bristol) and Laira (Plymouth). The majority of these run with the standard Western Region arrangement of seven trailers, but the Laira-based sets generally include an extra standard-class vehicle and also have a Trailer Restaurant Unclassified Buffet (TRUB) catering vehicle in place of the less well-equipped Trailer Restaurant Buffet (TRB) or Trailer Restaurant Standard Buffet (TRSB) vehicle of the other sets. Diagramming is complicated, especially because the Laira sets are required to work not only the long-distance West Country services but also certain peak business trains on other routes. Some IC125 units accumulate very high mileages: in summer 1988 the Pullman set used on the Penzance and Stratford-upon-Avon services was covering 856 miles a day.

A small number of locomotive-hauled trains remain in operation on WR InterCity services. These include Fridays-only departures to Bristol, Swansea and Plymouth, together with two Sunday trains each way on the Hereford line and a handful of workings to and from the West Country, again more on Sundays than during the week. To haul these trains the Western Region maintains a small stud of InterCity-liveried Class 47 locomotives, based at Bristol Bath Road where facilities can be shared with traction used on cross-country services. The identities of the WR domestic InterCity locomotives in late 1988 were 47560, 47611, 47613 and 47621.

BR's InterCity Cross-Country sub-Sector deals with a wide range of long-distance services on a broadly north-south axis, mostly routed via Birmingham New Street. The characteristics of this group of services are very different from those of the Western Region domestic services discussed earlier. Whereas on the London-Bristol and London-Cardiff routes a large proportion of BR's income is generated from first-class business travellers, this is not the case on the cross-country routes, where many passengers are optional customers, holding 'Saver' and other reduced price tickets. This meant that the case for including the cross-country services in the InterCity sub-Sector in the first place was a marginal one and major new investment is harder to justify here than for London-based routes.

Traditionally the main cross-country services were those on the northeast/northwest-south/southwest axis, but during the 1980s a number of innovations were made in order to serve a wider variety of destinations and attract new business from hitherto untapped markets. Looking first at services to and from the Northeast and Yorkshire, the weekday schedule for winter 1988-89 shows a

Left:
The monotony of Sprinters on the Cotswold line between Oxford and Worcester is relieved on weekdays by three InterCity 125 services in each direction. Pulling away from the attractive location of Moreton-in-Marsh on 29 August 1988 is the 14.13 InterCity 125 from Worcester Shrub Hill to London Paddington. The leading power car carries set number 253028; it is common practice on the Western Region to apply the unit number to the nose ends of IC125 units, even though the trains do not in practice run in fixed formations. *Paul Shannon*

basic frequency of between hourly and two-hourly, representing an improvement over previous years. This has been achieved partly by the provision of extra workings over the central sections of the route (eg Leeds-Birmingham) in order to fill the gaps left by the principal long-distance trains. One train in each direction serves Poole, and the remainder serve either South Wales (now via Bristol Parkway instead of via Chepstow) or the West Country. At the northern end InterCity has abandoned the shortest route (in terms of mileage) between Sheffield and York, so that trains to and from the Northeast may serve either Doncaster or Leeds en route. Most trains are IC125 units, but Class 47/4 haulage is used on the Poole train, the 'short' workings over the central portion of the route, and one service to and from Bristol.

For several years Manchester enjoyed the benefits of an InterCity 125 service on the northwest-southwest axis, a somewhat curious arrangement bearing in mind that diesel traction was running 'under the wires' for approximately 80 miles in each direction. This service was withdrawn in May 1988, but an IC125 unit was still booked to run similar distances over electrified lines to Liverpool and back in the winter 1988-89 timetable. With this sole exception, all trains between Scotland/Northwest England and the Southwest/South Coast are formed by locomotive and coaches, with the changeover between diesel and electric traction normally taking place at Birmingham New Street or Coventry. Four services in each direction are extended over the West Coast main line to and from Glasgow and Edinburgh, splitting at Carstairs. This splitting would not, of course be practicable if a unit train such as the IC125 were used. The recent increase in the number of InterCity cross-country services between Crewe and Scotland, together with an

increase to four daily workings between Manchester and Glasgow/Edinburgh, has compensated for the slight decline in the number of Euston-Glasgow trains, so that a roughly hourly service is still offered over the northern half of the West Coast main line. The weekday train covering the greatest distance in the winter 1988-89 timetable is the 'Devon Scot', taking 12hr 31min (southbound) or 12hr 48min (northbound) to travel 647 miles between Aberdeen and Plymouth. This record is exceeded on Sundays by the 08.10 Glasgow Central-Penzance which, as a consequence of West Coast main line engineering work and BR's determination not to use the Settle & Carlisle route for diversions, takes no less than 15hr 28min to reach its destination by way of Edinburgh, Newcastle, Doncaster and Sheffield. One of the features of cross-country services to/from the southwest is the large volume of holiday traffic which justifies the running of extra trains at weekends in summertime, especially on Saturdays. With an ever-tightening squeeze on resources BR is

Below:
During summer 1988 an 09.19 Bristol-York relief working regularly produced the combination of an InterCity-liveried Class 47 and Network SouthEast coaching stock, the latter borrowed from the Thames Valley fleet. This train is pictured near Water Orton on 9 July, headed by Class 47/4 No 47637 *Springburn*. *Peter Tandy*

Below right:
Still carrying the standard rail blue of corporate image days, Class 86/2 No 86230 *The Duke of Wellington* speeds past Springs Branch depot with the 13.40 Blackpool North-London Euston service on 2 August 1988. The stock on this occasion is a mixture of Mk 3 first-class and Mk 2F standard-class vehicles. *Paul Shannon*

less willing now than in former times to maintain large quantities of extra rolling stock (and extra locomotives) for such services, but is clearly keen to stay in the market for such traffic as far as possible and in May 1988 introduced a new IC125 service from Glasgow to Newquay together with locomotive-hauled trains from Rose Grove (Burnley) and Bolton to Paignton and Poole respectively.

One feature which all InterCity's cross-country services have in common is that they avoid the London termini. In May 1986 this concept was extended to a new group of services running via Kensington Olympia between northern England and coastal destinations in Kent and Sussex. Kensington Olympia had previously been used only as a Motorail terminal. A total of seven services in each direction was provided, bringing locomotive-hauled InterCity trains to Dover (four arrivals, three departures), Brighton (two arrivals and three departures) and Newhaven (one arrival and one departure). Unfortunately the Newhaven service was poorly patronised from the start and, with the gradual decline in the number of foot passengers on cross-Channel ferries, the loadings on the Dover trains were also disappointing. From May 1988 the service via Kensington Olympia was cut back to three trains in each direction. These were: the 'Sussex Scot' which ran between Brighton and Glasgow/Edinburgh; a service between Manchester and Brighton via the West Coast main line; and a service between Liverpool and Folkestone via Birmingham and the Thames Valley.

The resources for InterCity cross-country services in late 1988 included 12 IC125 units, based at St Philip's Marsh and Laira depots. In line with the comparatively small number of first-class passengers travelling on cross-country routes, the units have only one first-class trailer in contrast to the two included in Western Region domestic and East Coast main line formations. The sub-Sector also makes extensive use of hauled stock, mainly air-conditioned Mk 2 coaches based at Longsight (Manchester) and Polmadie (Glasgow). A fleet of 35 Class 47/4 locomotives is designated to haul the trains over non-electrified lines, divided between depots at Bristol Bath Road, Crewe and Eastfield, whilst Classes 86, 87 and 90 are used on the electrified West Coast main line. For summer Saturday extras locomotives and stock may be borrowed from other sectors, sometimes resulting in some intriguing combinations of liveries.

The West Coast main line qualifies as Europe's busiest trunk railway. Headways out of London Euston for InterCity services alone can be as little as 3min during peak periods, and on top of this the line carries a heavy complement of suburban passenger, freight and parcels traffic, particularly at its southern end. In the 1960s and early 1970s the West Coast main line was one of the principal beneficiaries of investment in infrastructure, traction and rolling stock on BR: it was the first long-distance route to be electrified, and one of the earliest applications of multiple-aspect signalling on a large scale. This is perhaps hardly surprising, bearing in mind the size of the conurbations situated on or near its main axis: no other London terminal than Euston serves a market as vast as that provided by the West Midlands, the industrial Northwest and Glasgow. Yet during the late 1970s and early 1980s the West Coast main line went through a period of comparative neglect, receiving little in the way of new investment by comparison with other InterCity routes. Whilst speeds were being increased to 125mph on the parallel East Coast route and on lines to Bristol and South Wales,

travellers on the West Coast main line are still faced with a basically 100mph service, with just a few trains permitted to run at up to 110mph. The signalling and trackwork on the West Coast main line now seems antiquated in comparison with that of other prime InterCity routes: even the neighbouring and much maligned Midland main line has more modern equipment than that in use between London and Crewe. The apparent neglect of BR's busiest main line is due at least in part to the failure of the Advanced Passenger Train project, since this at one time was considered to be the sole option for significantly enhancing train speeds on the WCML and thus offering a more attractive service to the passenger. Now at last, in the late 1980s, new equipment is beginning to appear on the West Coast main line. The first of the Class 90 electric locomotives was outshopped from Crewe in October 1987, with a view to squadron service during the 1988-89 timetable. A new build of 52 driving van trailers would be introduced at the same time as the Class 90s, enabling quicker turnrounds at termini and a net saving of 10 locomotives which would otherwise be 'locked' at the buffer stops. The 1990s will bring a much-needed new lease of life to West Coast InterCity services.

The most frequent workings out of London Euston are those to the West Midlands. A half-hourly frequency prevails as far as Birmingham, with alternate trains going through to Wolverhampton and six trains extended from Wolverhampton to Shrewsbury. Next in order of importance comes the London-Manchester service, with hourly trains operating in each direction for most of the day. Manchester trains may be routed either via Crewe or via Stoke-on-Trent, with broadly similar end-to-end timings over the two routes. The fastest down working in the winter 1988-89 schedule was the 08.00 Euston-Manchester via Crewe, taking 2hr 26min and the fastest up train was the 07.05 Manchester-Euston via Stoke, just slightly faster at 2hr 25min. Liverpool has not justified as lavish a service as Manchester in recent years and trains run approximately every one and a half hours on this route. The Euston-Glasgow service has been cut back, too, as a result of the airlines taking much of the BR's crucial first-class business traffic, although the 1988-89 schedule of six daytime London-Glasgow trains each way is made up to a roughly hourly frequency north of Preston by trains from the InterCity Cross-Country sub-Sector. Preston enjoys a good service to London, too, with its 15 trains in each direction provided by the sum total of Euston-Glasgow, Euston-Carlisle, Euston-Lancaster, Euston-Blackpool and Euston-Preston workings. The North Wales coast is served by five through trains to and from Euston on weekdays. Two of these connect with Sealink sailings to Dun Laoghaire and are designated the 'Irish Mail'. Returning to Scotland, Glasgow is not the only destination for West Coast main line services: in addition to the cross-country workings mentioned earlier, there is

the daily 'Clansman' service from London Euston to Inverness and Aberdeen. The whole train now runs via Edinburgh instead of via Motherwell and Coatbridge, and provides a direct link between London and Inverness on a schedule of 10hr 56min (southbound) or 10hr 35min (northbound). In both directions the 'Clansman' avoids the direct Rugby-Stafford line and takes the longer route through Birmingham and Wolverhampton, in order to provide the maximum range of through journey possibilities for the leisure market at which it is aimed. Whilst commanding the lion's share of ac traction resources on the West Coast main line, the InterCity Sector also makes use of a small fleet of Crewe-based Class 47/4 diesels, needed to operate trains to and from Shrewsbury, Holyhead and Blackpool. For diesel working north of the border, Eastfield also maintains a small fleet of Class 47/4s.

The Midland main line from London St Pancras to Derby, Nottingham and Sheffield has long been regarded as the poor relation of both East Coast and West Coast routes, with sizeable pockets of mechanical signalling around Leicester surviving into the mid-1980s and generally uninspiring line speeds over most of its length. The line did receive a major boost in October 1982, however, when IC125 units were drafted in from other routes in sufficient quantities to quickly become the mainstay of the line's service. By October 1988 only two locomotive-hauled passenger services remained in operation south of Leicester; these were a daily 'peak hour' working from Derby to London and back, and a Friday afternoon working from Derby to London to provide an extra evening departure from St Pancras to Derby. Thirteen InterCity 125 sets were employed on Midland main line duties in late 1988, all based for maintenance purposes at Leeds Neville Hill. They provide a basic half-hourly service between St Pancras and Leicester, beyond which point the route divides for Nottingham or Derby. Some trains terminate at Leicester, whilst the others continue north to provide a train every 90min both to Nottingham and to Sheffield via Derby. The Nottingham route is less attractive as a through route to Sheffield because it involves a reversal and (if Lenton-Trowell were to be closed) a lengthy diversion via Beeston and Toton, but two Sheffield-London and one London-Sheffield workings still

Above right:
One of the first Class 87 locomotives to carry the InterCity Swallow livery, No 87028 *Lord President*, heads north with the 07.57 Plymouth-Liverpool Lime Street service near Whitmore on 29 October 1988. *Paul Shannon*

Right:
One of the more trouble-free members of Class 90 in the early stages was No 90004, which was frequently used on passenger turns during the summer of 1988. No 90004 is pictured on one of its successful runs on 16 August, leaving Crewe with the 14.30 service from London Euston to Glasgow Central. The photograph is taken from the viewing area on the roof of the old Crewe North signalbox, now part of Crewe Heritage Centre. *Hugh Ballantyne*

Above:
The first Class 90 to be outshopped from Crewe, No 90001, began its career by hauling test trains on the West Coast main line in January 1988. Here No 90001 approaches Rugby with the 10.10 Crewe-Willesden working on 17 February 1988. The formation consists of one Railway Technical Centre test coach, five ex-works Mk 3A Restaurant Buffet First conversions (Nos 10254 to 10258) and Mk 3B Open Brake First No 17174. *David Rapson*

Right:
Class 85 No 85015 passes Wigan with 1M69, the 11.40 MWFO Motorail service from Stirling to London Euston, on 31 August 1988. This summer-only working was the last Motorail service to use open Carflats, and by 1988 was also one of the last vacuum-braked passenger trains on the West Coast main line. A noteworthy addition to the dedicated rake of Mk 1 FKs is a Network SouthEast-liveried brake vehicle! *Paul Shannon*

run via Nottingham in order to serve Alfreton & Mansfield Parkway. At the northern end of the route, one InterCity 125 service in each direction is extended to/from Barnsley, and another to/from Leeds and (southbound only) Bradford Forster Square.

If on the West Coast main line business between London and Scotland has declined as a consequence of competition from air travel, the same can certainly not be said of the equivalent East Coast route. The London-Edinburgh link is very much the flagship of InterCity operations on the East Coast

main line, and enough custom is generated to justify an hourly service between the two capitals throughout the day. The principal reason for the difference in fortunes between the East and West Coast routes is the IC125 unit, which from 1978 onwards has brought significant reductions in journey times and improvements in service quality between London and Edinburgh. The fastest timings for the 393-mile journey are, in the winter 1988-89 schedule, 4hr 25min in the southbound direction (on the 10.30 'Flying Scotsman' from Edinburgh) and 4hr 23min in the northbound direction (on the 10.30 'Flying Scotsman' from King's Cross). These are a good 40min faster than the equivalent 'best' services on the West Coast route. Partly because of the higher speeds attainable, but also because of the existence of a through station at Edinburgh (in contrast to Glasgow), the East Coast route carries the greater proportion of through trains between London and the North of Scotland. Aberdeen is the principal starting point and destination for such trains and enjoys a weekday service of four services in each direction. The fastest of these is the 10.30 'Flying Scotsman' from King's Cross (again!), scheduled to cover the 524 miles to Aberdeen in 6hr 54min. Another pair of services runs over the Highland main line to/from Inverness, calling at Stirling and Perth en route, and bettering the 'Clansman' schedule between London and Inverness by a margin of 2½hr. Glasgow Queen Street, too, has a direct rail link with King's Cross, comprising two southbound workings on weekday mornings and two return trains from London in the afternoon.

Within 150 miles of London the East Coast main line serves fewer large population centres than its partner based on Euston. The likes of Grantham, Newark and Retford, even with the recent upsurge in long-distance commuter traffic to London, do not really stand comparison with the densely populated West Midlands corridor stretching from Coventry through Birmingham to Wolverhampton. From Doncaster northwards, however, there is enough business at intermediate stations to justify a number of 'short' workings supplementing the basic Anglo-Scottish service. Most of these start and finish at Newcastle (there are seven northbound and eight southbound of them on weekdays), and there is also one working each way to and from York. The principal offshoot from the main East Coast artery is Leeds, which commands an hourly service for most of the day to and from London. One Leeds working in each direction is extended to/from Harrogate, and Bradford is also served by one up and two down trains via Leeds. Until October 1988 the Bradford trains used the Great Northern route via New Pudsey to terminate at Interchange, but now they run over former Midland tracks to Shipley and into the much rationalised terminus at Forster Square. The move was made with a view to capturing new custom from businessmen in the prosperous Aire Valley; little first-class traffic was ever generated at New Pudsey. Cleethorpes and Hull retain one and two direct London trains

respectively, whilst Middlesbrough, Hartlepool and Sunderland are served by the 'Cleveland Executive' in each direction. The southbound 'Cleveland Executive' is now the only scheduled passenger train to traverse the Northallerton-Eaglescliffe line; the northbound working reverses at Darlington.

For East Coast main line services a fleet of 34 IC125 units is shared between maintenance depots at Bounds Green (London), Neville Hill (Leeds) and Craigentinny (Edinburgh). All are 2+8 formations, in contrast to the 2+7 pattern prevailing on Western Region and Cross-Country services. The electrification currently under way will, of course, bring major changes to the East Coast route, and by the end of 1988 the first examples of the new Class 91 'Electra' locomotives were becoming a common sight on test trains on the main line. At one point it had been hoped to introduce the '91s' into revenue-earning service in October 1988, one year ahead of the original schedule. This proved to be over-optimistic in view of persistent teething troubles with the new technology, but the first scheduled passenger-carrying runs were still made ahead of time in March 1989. Meanwhile the sole Brush-designed Class 89 prototype, the traction type on which the original case for East Coast

electrification had been based in July 1984, was biding its time on commuter trains out of King's Cross: it took up regular duties on the 07.00 from Peterborough and the 17.36 return during July 1988.

BR's newest region, the Anglia Region, is host to InterCity services on the London-Norwich corridor, including the Harwich branch. An hourly service is maintained throughout the day to Norwich, and there are three down and two up InterCity services between Liverpool Street and Harwich Parkeston Quay. Intermediate stations between London and Colchester are generally served only by Network SouthEast trains. Electrification reached Ipswich in May 1985, and Norwich itself gained its full electric service on 5 May 1987, a day marked by the appropriate ceremonials and by the renaming of No 86220 as *The Round Tabler*. With the new service came a small but significant saving in average journey time between London and Norwich, helping to boost further the already buoyant traffic on this route. Haulage is provided exclusively by Class 86/2 locomotives, based at Ilford instead of Willesden since March 1989, and the passenger accommodation consists of late Mk 2 air-conditioned stock. After the commissioning of the North London line electrification scheme in early 1988, it became possible for the 86/2s to move between Willesden and Great Eastern metals under their own power. On 18 April of that year the Harwich-Glasgow/Edinburgh 'European' became the first InterCity passenger service to be diagrammed for electric haulage over the North London line, but this operation lasted only a few weeks since the train was withdrawn after the timetable change of 14 May.

The only domestic InterCity service on the Southern Region is the 'Gatwick Express'. With a distance of barely 27 miles and a journey time of

Below:
In connection with InterCity's 21st birthday celebrations in May 1987, 'AL6' (Class 86) locomotive No 86426 was restored to an approximation of its 1966 livery and given its former number E3195. It was coupled to a rake of maroon Mk 1 stock for its festive journey, a choice which seemed inappropriate to purists since the coaching stock used on London-Manchester services in 1966 would actually have included the latest blue and grey Mk 2 vehicles. Nevertheless the combination of blue and maroon was an eye-catching one, as shown in this view of E3195 on a special Carlisle-Euston run on 25 July 1987. *Douglas Johnson*

only 30min between Victoria and Gatwick Airport, this service may seem a surprising candidate for InterCity status. On the other hand, the spread of clientèle gives the 'Gatwick Express' greater similarity to Euston-Birmingham than to the Network SouthEast empire which surrounds it, and certainly as far as distance is concerned the 'Gatwick Express' is, for the majority of passengers, a stepping stone for a much longer journey! The 'Gatwick Express' as it exists today was launched in May 1984, using an ingenious combination of modern rolling stock and not-so-modern traction to replace the makeshift 4-VEG units which had operated the service since 1978. The passenger accommodation now comprises semi-permanently coupled sets of Mk 2f carriages, adapted from locomotive-hauled vehicles with a modified seating layout and extra luggage space, and these are sandwiched between a single Class 73 electro-diesel at one end (normally the Gatwick end) and a converted ex-Class 414 driving trailer at the other. The service is one of the most intensive on the BR system, with departures from Victoria every 15min daily from 05.30 until 22.00, and two later departures at 22.30 and 23.00. During the night a roughly hourly service is provided on this route by Network SouthEast.

Despite the introduction of new Mk 3 vehicles in the early 1980s, business on BR's sleeper services has declined steadily over the past decade. InterCity is perhaps a victim of its own success here, insofar as the decline is attributed partly to the acceleration of daytime services on prime routes: it is now possible to leave Newcastle at 05.50 and reach King's Cross at 08.59, for example, and many passengers would prefer this arrangement to one involving a departure on the previous evening. The biggest and boldest step taken in the sleeper business for many a year was the total

abandonment of the East Coast route in May 1988. There were, of course, many complaints from travellers to and from areas now deprived of their service, from Darlington through Newcastle to Dunbar, and BR agreed to reappraise the matter after the completion of East Coast main line (ECML) electrification in 1991. For the time being, however, all London-Scotland sleeper services are now concentrated on the West Coast route and use Euston as their London terminus. This arrangement is seen as advantageous in several respects: it allows electric haulage to replace the more costly Class 47s used on the East Coast route; passenger facilities can be concentrated at one London terminus; facilities for stock cleaning and maintenance at the London end can similarly be rationalised; and, last but not least, the West Coast main line can handle trains several coaches longer than the maximum permitted at King's Cross. In the winter 1988-89 timetable there were seven trains in each direction between Euston and Scotland; northbound these departed from Euston between 20.20 and 23.50 whilst southbound trains are timed to arrive between 04.46 and 08.14. Many sleeper trains convey portions which are attached or detached en route, and the winter 1988/89 timetable included joint services to Stranraer and Inverness (splitting at Carstairs), Edinburgh and Glasgow (splitting at Carstairs) and to Aberdeen and Fort William (splitting at Mossend). Manchester and Liverpool retain their overnight rail link with London, and in the up direction portions from these two cities are combined with a one-way working from Barrow-in-Furness. On the Western Region the 'Night Riviera' provides sleeping car accommodation between Paddington and Penzance, and Plymouth is also reached by one arm of BR's only cross-country sleeper service. The latter is a relatively recent development for BR and

Right:
A second direct link between London and Inverness, albeit slower than the 'Highland Chieftain', is the daily 'Clansman' service to and from Euston. Slochd viaduct forms a majestic setting for the southbound 'Clansman', the 11.00 departure from Inverness, on 12 March 1987. The motive power is Class 47/4 No 47604, which at that time would have remained in charge of the train as far as Mossend yard. An Edinburgh portion would then be added at Carstairs. In May 1987 the main 'Clansman' train was re-routed via Edinburgh, with a portion detached or attached at Carstairs for Motherwell and Glasgow.
John Chalcraft

Above left:
**When sections of the West Coast main line are blocked by
Sunday engineering work and diversions are in operation
over non-electrified routes, it is common for the rostered
electric locomotive to be piloted by diesel traction. On
15 June 1986, No 87003 is piloted by Class 47 No 47551 as it
passes Lostock Junction with the 09.45 London Euston-
Glasgow Central service. The train in this instance had left
its normal route at Crewe and had travelled via Stockport,
Ashton Moss, Manchester Victoria and Bolton, before
regaining familiar WCML metals at Euxton Junction. Now
that the Windsor Link is open, a less circuitous route
through Manchester is possible.** *Paul Shannon*

Left:
**A number of Mk 1 FOs were given a fresh lease of life in the
mid-1980s when they were acquired by the InterCity
charter fleet. The vehicles concerned were extensively
refurbished and repainted in InterCity livery before taking
up their duties from Bounds Green depot. Since 1986 they
have regularly been used on the 'Highlander' and 'West
Highlander' weekend excursions from London. A working
of the 'West Highlander' is illustrated descending Glen
Falloch on Sunday 28 June 1987, with traction provided by
recently-named Class 37/4 No 37412** *Loch Lomond.*
Gavin Morrison

Above:
**The intricate trackwork at the south end of York station is
picked out by the evening sunshine as the 14.35 Edinburgh-
King's Cross InterCity 125 service pulls away after making
its scheduled stop on 17 October 1987. York was one of the
few locations on the East Coast main line where major
trackwork and signalling renewal was necessary before
electrification work could start in earnest.** *Michael Rhodes*

provides through coaches between Glasgow and
Edinburgh in the north and Plymouth and Poole in
the south. Within Scotland, an overnight train with
sleeper accommodation connects Glasgow and
Edinburgh with Inverness, and there is also a
one-way service from Glasgow to Aberdeen.

One category of regular passenger workings that
does not feature in the public timetable is the set of
car-carrying trains marketed under the name
Motorail. With the decline in popularity of this
mode of transport, the days of a comprehensive
Motorail network are over, and only a small number
of services are now operated. Kensington Olympia
has relinquished its role as a Motorail terminal in
preference to the shared use of Euston and
Paddington for London trains. Year-round services
operate from Euston to Carlisle, Edinburgh,
Aberdeen and Inverness, from Paddington to
Penzance and from Bristol to Edinburgh, together
with return journeys. An extra summer-only
service operates between Paddington and Penzance,
and until 1988 another seasonal train ran between
Euston and Stirling, the latter being the last train to
use traditional Motorail Carflats for its vehicle-
carrying portion.

The InterCity Sector oversees a variety of charter
train operations, and for the enthusiast these
continue to provide some welcome relief from the
increasing monotony of IC125 units and Sprinters
on so many of BR's principal routes. The special

trains programme has changed in the past decade or so from a flexible and in some ways amorphous extension of scheduled services to a tightly controlled set of workings aimed at specific markets. In the 1970s BR seemed only too happy to use the vast numbers of spare Mk 1 coaches and freight locomotives to run weekend excursions at knock-down prices — the writer recalls travelling from Watford to Carlisle and back in 1973 for the princely sum of 25p! In the 1980s things are very different, given the more businesslike approach that BR has had to adopt in order to bring its InterCity operations into profit. Spare coaching stock and traction has largely been eliminated from the system, and everything that remains is used as efficiently as possible by the specific sub-Sector to which it is allotted. Nevertheless, the special trains business on BR is far from dead; on the contrary it now commands its own resources, including an allocation of locomotives and rolling stock, within

Left:
With its first 10 years of service behind it and with its East Coast main line duties soon to come to an end, Class 43 power car No 43062 heads a standard rake of ECML InterCity 125 vehicles through Knebworth on 23 August 1988, forming the 13.00 Leeds-King's Cross service.
Paul Shannon

Below left:
One of the remaining 'Generators', Class 47/4 No 47413, draws a rake of empty air-conditioned Mk 2 coaches into King's Cross Goods for the purpose of running round on 3 November 1988. All InterCity services on the southern part of the East Coast main line are now operated by IC125 units (or their successors the Class 91), and the appearance of a Class 47 with passenger stock so near to the terminus is now something of a rarity. The locomotive pictured here was one of three Class 47/4s allocated to Settle-Carlisle line duties in November 1988. The lines to King's Cross passenger station lead off to the right, and the North London line is also visible running from left to right at the top of the picture. *Paul Shannon*

Above:
The prototype Brush Class 89, No 89001, made its first run in passenger service on the East Coast main line on 3 July 1988, when it hauled a special from King's Cross to Doncaster. Soon afterwards it took up a regular duty on a peak-hour diagram from and to Peterborough, with occasional workings to and from Leeds. In this picture, taken on 4 November 1988, No 89001 is flanked by already outmoded InterCity 125 units at King's Cross as it awaits departure with the 17.36 to Peterborough. *Paul Shannon*

Below:
Shortly after receiving a full repaint in InterCity livery and acquiring the name *Avocet*, Brush Class 89 No 89001 enters Leeds City station on 21 January 1989 with one of the InterCity 'Thames-Eden' charter specials. The train was taken forward from Leeds to Carlisle by green-liveried Class 45 No 45106. *Gavin Morrison*

Above:
GEC and BR confounded many of their critics in February 1988 when the first Class 91 locomotive emerged from the BREL workshops at Crewe precisely on schedule. No 91001 is illustrated here on the day of its presentation to the media, 12 February, providing a first glimpse of what will become standard traction for the electrified East Coast main line. The 'blunt' end nearest the camera will normally be positioned next to the first/last carriage in a push-pull formation, but can also be used as a front driving position when the locomotive is working freight or parcels services. *Hugh Ballantyne*

Below:
By autumn 1988 Class 91s were making frequent appearances on test trains and driver training specials on the East Coast main line, although the onetime ambition to press them into revenue-earning service a year early had not been fulfilled. No 91003 leaves Leeds City blunt end first with a test train for Peterborough on 13 October 1988.
Gavin Morrison

the InterCity organisation as a whole. The bulk of the InterCity charter fleet is made up of late-built Mk 1 carriages displaced from scheduled services by more modern stock, whilst it also includes a batch of Mk 3 sleepers, some Mk 2 seating vehicles and ten former 'Manchester Pullman' cars. A number of liveries are carried, ranging from LNER green and cream through 1960s maroon and standard blue and grey to the latest 'raspberry ripple' InterCity colour scheme. To some extent there is an overlap between resources intended for charter trains and those intended for seasonal or relief services: the Euston-Stirling Motorail carriages, for example, were used on charter work in winter. Amongst the most ambitious charter trains organised by BR have been the 'Scottish Land Cruises', which are basically three- or four-day excursions from London to a variety of destinations in the Highlands. The first 'Scottish Land Cruises' ran in 1986, using a colourful combination of InterCity-liveried Mk 1 seating coaches and Mk 3 sleepers. Using either St Pancras or King's Cross as

Above:
Staff at Tinsley depot made an excellent job of repainting Class 20 locomotives Nos 20030 and 20064 in BR green for the Class 20 Locomotive Society's 'Three to the Sea' railtour on 2 May 1987. The pair are pictured at Tinsley on 11 March 1987, also carrying the names *River Rother* and *River Sheaf* which were subsequently removed. *Gavin Morrison*

Left:
The working of the Royal Train is within the InterCity remit. Looking resplendent with silver roof, red buffer beams and white wheel rims, Class 47/4 No 47585 passes Low Moor with a working of the Royal Train on 6 February 1987, in this instance carrying Princess Diana to Bradford. *John S. Whiteley*

23

Above:
An interim stage in the Anglia electrification scheme was reached in May 1985 when Norwich services were diagrammed for electric haulage as far as Ipswich. Standing at Colchester on 6 August 1986 is Class 86/2 locomotive No 86222 *Fury*, heading the 11.30 departure from Liverpool Street. The name *Fury* was subsequently removed from No 86222 and replaced by the name *Lloyds List 250th Anniversary* during a ceremony at Colchester in June 1987. *Ian Gould*

Left:
Once the wires were extended all the way to Norwich, Anglia Region required the use of 16 Class 86/2 locomotives for its electrically-hauled services. On 24 July 1988 No 86216 *Meteor* passes Claydon, north of Ipswich, with the 16.20 service from London Liverpool Street to Norwich.
Michael J. Collins

their starting point, they have run either as the 'Highlander' to Kyle of Lochalsh and the Far North, or else as the 'West Highlander' to Oban and Mallaig. Following the model of the Scottish trains, but on a smaller scale, have been the 'Luxury Days Out' or 'Day Land Cruises' to destinations such as Penrith, Harrogate, Blaenau Ffestiniog and Lincoln. Supplementing the BR programme are trains owned and operated by private companies, of which the 'Venice-Simplon Orient Express' is probably the best known example. Indeed it was partly the success of the 'Royal Scotsman', another privately-owned touring train, which provided the impetus for the development of BR's own charter operations in the mid-1980s.

Twelve locomotives from Class 73/1 were dedicated to work only Gatwick Express services from February 1988 and were renumbered in the 732xx series accordingly. No 73204 *Stewarts Lane 1860-1985* passes Clapham Junction with a Gatwick-bound working on 6 August 1988.   *Geoff Cann*

CHAPTER TWO

Provincial

The Provincial Sector stretches literally from Penzance to Wick, and embraces the majority of BR's local and medium-distance passenger services outside the Southeast. It is one of the two sectors which is never expected to record a profit, and yet its financial performance has come under ever closer scrutiny in recent years in the face of successive reductions in subsidy paid by central government. Since 1983 Provincial has been able to reduce its operating costs substantially, whilst at the same time expanding its services and investing in large quantities of new rolling stock. Revenue from this sector's operations was over 7% higher in 1987-88 than in the previous financial year, with the ratio of operating costs to earnings decreasing steadily towards the target figure of 2½:1. Increased efficiency is the key to Provincial's success, and this will continue to be the sector's overriding concern in future years: if present objectives are to be met, the amount of government grant per passenger will need to fall by one-quarter between 1988 and 1993.

Since Provincial Sector was established in 1982, over 70 stations have been opened or reopened, ranging from small unstaffed halts such as Hall i'th'Wood (Bolton) and Roughton Road (Cromer) to the major Snow Hill revival in Birmingham. New railways have appeared on the map, too, either by bringing freight-only lines up to passenger standards or by entirely new construction. In the former category are Edinburgh-Bathgate, which reopened in March 1986 after a gap of 30 years, Nuneaton-Coventry, reopened in May 1987, the short but significant link from Birmingham Moor

Below:
The attractive station at Woodbridge has remained more or less intact to the present day, although none of the buildings are available for public use; indeed it is an unstaffed halt. It is also the end of the single-track section south from Saxmundham, signalled using Radio Electronic Token Block. The aerials on both the station building and the front of the Class 101 may be seen. The service illustrated is the 11.00 Lowestoft-Ipswich on 21 July 1988.
John Glover

Street to Snow Hill, reopened in October 1987, the Cardiff City line, also launched in October 1987, and the Aberdare branch, reopened to regular passenger trains in October 1988. New construction has included the Hazel Grove link, the Holmes Chord at Rotherham and the Windsor Link in Manchester, opened in May 1986, May 1987 and May 1988 respectively. Most of these schemes owe their success to the close partnership between BR and local authorities which has developed to varying degrees in different parts of the country. Another factor has been the so-called Speller Amendment of 1980, which made it possible for BR to withdraw a service that had been introduced on an experimental basis without going through the lengthy (and expensive) statutory closure procedure. Lest it be thought that all changes in Provincial infrastructure during the 1980s have been positive, it is important to mention the negative developments as well. Complete station or line closures have been few, and largely limited to minor instances of 'pruning' such as Balloch Pier and the Brindle Heath-Agecroft spur in Manchester. But in some parts of the country rationalisation of trackwork or signalling has had an adverse effect on train frequency or reliability, such as the track singling which has taken place on the Chester-Wrexham line and on the Blackpool South branch. And as the 1980s draw to a close, the prospect of some actual line closures in the next few years seems real, with the firm proposal made in October 1988 to withdraw passenger services from Gainsborough-Barnetby as a possible precursor of more general 'bustitution'.

One technological advance that has brightened the future of many rural lines is Radio Electronic Token Block signalling. This form of signalling, where electronic messages are passed directly between the control centre and locomotive cabs, enables one 'signalman' to remotely control the movements of several trains over a lengthy section of railway, without the need for traditional fixed signals. It has already been applied to a number of routes where traffic levels would never justify full multiple-aspect signalling, including the East Suffolk line, the Cambrian Coast line, the Far North line and the West Highland lines. On the West Highland lines alone, 16 mechanical signalboxes were superseded by the single control centre at Banavie when the scheme became fully operative in May 1988, leading to a significant reduction in BR's wages bill. One spin-off from RETB is the ability to run a handful of trains during the night without engaging an expensive night shift at numerous individual signalboxes: on the West Highland two out of the three freights in each direction have been retimed to travel partly or wholly during the night, enabling better use of resources and easier pathing of daytime passenger services.

In the past it has been common for traction and rolling stock to be passed down from top-ranking

Below:
Wrawby Junction lies just west of Barnetby and is the point where routes to Lincoln, Gainsborough and Scunthorpe diverge. Passing a fine set of bracket signals guarding the junction is one of the 50 Class 150/1 Sprinter units, forming a morning train to Cleethorpes on 6 May 1988.
John S. Whiteley

One route to regain locomotive haulage for a short spell during the 1980s was the Manchester-Sheffield line through the Hope Valley. The service using Class 31/4s and early Mk 2 coaching stock was launched in May 1984, and lasted until May 1988. On the final day of operation, 14 May 1988, Class 31/4 No 31448 is photographed near Hope with the 12.45 Liverpool Lime Street-Sheffield. The last carriage in the train is, unusually for this service, a late Mk 2 air-conditioned vehicle. *Brian Denton*

express duties to lesser suburban and rural ones in the course of time, so that Mk 1 coaches once used on Anglo-Scottish expresses would find themselves working between Bristol and Portsmouth or between Manchester and Hull. Now, the days of such 'cascading' seem to be over, at least as far as the Provincial Sector is concerned, and instead brand-new hardware is finding its way on to local and middle-distance services in all parts of the country. Locomotive haulage is being virtually abandoned by the Provincial Sector, which according to BR's 1988 Corporate Plan expects to require the use of only 10 locomotives by 1992-93. The brand-new hardware is the rapidly expanding fleet of second-generation diesel multiple-units, the Sprinters and Pacers, which offer a much cheaper and in some ways more flexible alternative to locomotives and hauled stock. In one instance, on the Manchester-Blackpool route, the anticipated

low running costs of Sprinters even resulted in the abandonment of an apparently attractive electrification scheme, one that could also have been of benefit to InterCity services and possibly to freight.

The 'Sprinter Revolution' proper began in January 1986, when Class 150/1 units were introduced in squadron service on lines radiating from the East Midlands. The entire fleet of 50 two-car units is based at Derby Etches Park, in line with BR policy to centralise rolling stock maintenance at fewer separate locations, but their sphere of operations is vast, stretching from Holyhead and Pwllheli in the west to Cleethorpes and Skegness in the east. The two-car configuration of the '150/1s', a feature shared by the majority of later 'Sprinter' types, enables BR to run shorter trains at more frequent intervals over certain routes, whilst in those areas where loadings are high, such as the Cambrian Coast line in summer, several two-car units can be coupled together. During 1988 a number of '150/1' units were augmented to three-car formation by the addition of a powered intermediate vehicle. Next off the production line after the '150/1s' were the '150/2s', similar in design to their predecessors but with end corridor connections and a revised seating layout. Visually the '150/2s' were also different in that they carried a revised version of the Provincial livery,

with the dark blue band at window height instead of at waist level. The first regular diagrams for Class 150/2 units began in March 1987, when two units replaced locomotive-hauled trains on the Holyhead-Scarborough run. The total build of 85 two-car units was divided between four maintenance depots, at Newton Heath, Neville Hill, Cardiff and Haymarket. Those based at Newton Heath work local services in the Manchester area, in some cases deputising for unavailable Pacers, and also services to Blackpool and North Wales. The Neville Hill allocation may be seen on local services around Leeds and also on Trans-Pennine services via Diggle. Class 150/2s allocated to Cardiff work mainly in the Valleys, whilst those based at Haymarket are diagrammed to work Edinburgh-Bathgate and Edinburgh-Dundee trains. There was some delay in commissioning the full Class 150/2 fleet, and this, coupled with chronic overcrowding on certain services during their first summer, brought BR under heavy criticism from travellers and press alike. On the other hand, substantial improvements to journey times were achieved, such as from 90min to 72min on the Edinburgh-Dundee run.

The two breeds of Class 150 'Sprinter' were largely brought in as replacements for existing multiple-unit stock. This was not the case with the next two varieties of 'Sprinter', the Leyland-built Class 155 and the Metro-Cammell-built Class 156. These were intended to replace locomotive-hauled

trains as well as first-generation DMUs. The design of Classes 155 and 156 differs from that of the Class 150/2 in several respects: Classes 155 and 156 have longer coach bodies (23m instead of 20m), more generously spaced seating (2+2 instead of 2+3) and fewer external doors. Both Classes 155 and 156 made their debut in revenue-earning service during 1987, but a more significant date was 16 May 1988, when BR's 'Sprinter Express' network was launched. Twenty-four out of the 35 Class 155 units based at Cardiff were diagrammed to work an hourly service on two fairly lengthy

With the first snowfall of the winter lending a seasonal flavour to the Pennine hills, Class 47/4 No 47434 passes Diggle signalbox with the 07.45 Newcastle-Liverpool Lime Street service on 20 November 1988. By this time almost all the early Mk 2 carriages used on North Trans-Pennine workings had been painted in Provincial colours. No 47434 was named *Pride in Huddersfield* at a ceremony in Huddersfield itself on 16 June 1988.
Paul Shannon

Above left:
It was condemned at Carlisle in August 1981 but then reinstated for a further five years' main line service — English Electric Class 40 No 40122, or D200 as it was more usually called, was a remarkable machine which attracted a considerable enthusiast following during its prolonged life. In between working charter trains to many remote corners of the BR network, D200 spent several summers plying between Leeds and Carlisle on scheduled services, adding a further source of attraction to what was already one of the most scenic journeys on BR. It is pictured passing the rare splitting distant signal at Apperley Junction, between Shipley and Leeds, with the 10.40 train from Carlisle on 14 July 1986.
Paul Shannon

Below left:
The last six members of the 25-strong Class 143 fleet were outshopped in the Tyne & Wear PTE colours of yellow and white. No 143024 pulls away from the down platform at Hexham with the 11.51 departure to Sunderland via Newcastle on 28 February 1987. The Tyne Valley line through Hexham was one of the routes promoted in 1986 under the 'Britain's Scenic Railways' banner, and despite major problems with the Class 143 rolling stock the line was to witness a pleasing increase in patronage.
Douglas Johnson

Right:
It is probably fair to say that ScotRail takes a greater pride in its stations than many other administrations on BR. The station at Wemyss Bay is one which retains much of its period charm. It is pictured on 7 April 1988 with Class 303 unit No 303054 in attendance, waiting to form an evening service to Glasgow Central. *Les Nixon*

Above:

Eastfield depot on 4 September 1988, with a varied selection of ScotRail traction on show in the yard. From left to right are Class 47/4s Nos 47617 *University of Stirling* and 47622 *The Institution of Mechanical Engineers*, Class 26 No 26032, Class 47/4 No 47595 *Confederation of British Industry*, Class 37/4 No 37408 *Loch Rannoch*, and Class 20s Nos 20192 and 20138. Eastfield is by far the largest locomotive depot on ScotRail, having responsibility for approximately 250 locomotives spread across all BR's business sectors except Network SouthEast. *Gavin Morrison*

Left:

Class 47 motive power was the order of the day for Glasgow-Stranraer passenger workings until the Sprinter revolution reached these parts in October 1988. On 27 June 1988, No 47146 departs from Stranraer Harbour station with the 07.00 service to Glasgow Central, comprising just four Mk 1 carriages. In the background the Sealink vessel *St David* leaves the harbour with the 07.00 sailing to Larne. *Jeremy Hunns*

the Metro-Cammell Class 101 and the Derby 'Lightweight' Class 108, but there were also significant numbers of Derby 'Suburban' Class 116 and Birmingham RC&W Class 104 units remaining in service. The West Midlands is one particular area where traditional DMUs abound, with no immediate prospects of replacement by Sprinters or other more modern stock. One notable feature of the late 1980s has been the mixing of different vehicle types within units, and also the reallocation of certain types to parts of the country where they had hardly ever been seen before. Class 104s were moved from their familiar stamping grounds in the Northwest to less familiar pastures in both Scotland and London, with individual Class 104 cars often coupled up to 'foreign' units. Two-car Class 108 units were sent to Bristol, and the West Midlands

Above:

Although primarily intended for Glasgow-Edinburgh work, the 16-strong fleet of Class 47/7s has seen regular employment on services between Glasgow and Aberdeen. With its ScotRail livery matching that of the rolling stock in its wake, No 47707 *Holyrood* crosses the River Forth as it approaches Stirling on 3 June 1986, forming the 17.00 express from Aberdeen. *W. A. Sharman*

Right:

Negotiating the famous Horseshoe Curve between Bridge of Orchy and Tyndrum on 9 April 1988 are Class 37/4 locomotives Nos 37403 *Isle of Mull* and 37423, providing ample power for the 08.30 Fort William-Glasgow Queen Street service. No 37403 carries the standard 'revised blue' or 'large logo' livery once carried by all Class 37/4s, whilst No 37423 was the first member of the sub-class to be painted in the new three-tone grey Railfreight colour scheme. In May 1988 No 37423 was further embellished with Metals sub-Sector markings and named *Sir Murray Morrison 1874-1948* (pioneer of the British aluminium industry) in honour of the new contract for railborne alumina traffic to Fort William. *Les Nixon*

received a small influx of suburban units from Network SouthEast, breaking the Western Region's hold on the Pressed Steel Class 117s. Many of these changes were the indirect result of BR's obligation to withdraw asbestos-contaminated stock.

As for locomotive haulage, this continues to diminish with each successive timetable change, but 1988 saw hauled stock survive longer than planned on a number of routes as a result of problems with Pacers or late delivery of Sprinters. In the Northeast, Class 47s and Mk 1 coaches were deputising for Pacers on several Newcastle area diagrams, bringing locomotive haulage to the Tyne Valley and to the coast line via Sunderland. The continuing problems with Class 142 Pacers in the Northwest led to the use of Classes 31 and 47 on Blackpool trains, with occasional forays to Blackburn and Southport. And on the Western Region, the late delivery and subsequent withdrawal of the Class 155 Sprinters saw Class 37/4s hauling trains on the Marches line well into 1989, as well as Class 47/4s operating between Bristol and Taunton for a while. Most of the locomotives used on these services had to be

Above:
The Caithness termini of Thurso and Wick are similar in many respects, both retaining their simple but attractive Highland Railway train sheds. On 30 June 1987, Class 37/4 No 37418 spends its layover time at Thurso in between working trains to and from Georgemas Junction. After the planned arrival of the Sprinters on the Far North Line in January 1989 BR had intended to continue diagramming a Class 37/4 for Thurso branch workings, utilising the Georgemas ballast locomotive which would otherwise spend much of its time idle. *Gavin Morrison*

Left:
Class 37/4 No 37412 *Loch Lomond* **stands at Oban with empty coaching stock on the evening of 28 September 1987, ready to work the following day's 08.00 departure to Glasgow.** *Ian Gould*

borrowed from other sectors. Provincial's own locomotive fleet consisted of 17 Class 37/4s, 25 Class 47/4s and all 16 Class 47/7s in late 1988. The '37s' were divided between Inverness for Far North and Kyle line services, Eastfield for the West Highland line, and Cardiff for Cambrian duties. The present usage of locomotives on through trains to the Cambrian Coast dates back only to April 1986, when Barmouth Bridge was declared fit once again to take the weight of '37s'. A pool of nine Class 47/4s was allocated to Crewe for the two-hourly Newcastle-Liverpool Trans-Pennine workings, and in November 1988 three Class 47/4s were based at Immingham for use on the Settle-Carlisle line. In Scotland, Inverness had responsibility for Provincial's fleet of Class 47/4s, whilst Eastfield maintained the push-pull fitted Class 47/7s, used mainly on Edinburgh-Glasgow expresses. Provincial's plans will see virtually all of these services go over to Sprinter operation in due course, mostly using the fleet of 194 luxury Class 158 vehicles which was ordered in November 1987. The last bastions of locomotive haulage on Provincial services will probably be seasonal holiday trains, using traction borrowed from the Railfreight Sector. Regular passenger duties for freight or departmental locomotives in 1988, apart from the 'emergency' cases listed above, included 'Buxton stone' Class 37/5s on the Cambrian, Class 20s to Skegness and Class 31/4s on a Hull-Holyhead diagram.

Left:
Scenery that is truly hard to beat! Class 37/4 No 37416 runs alongside Loch Carron on 5 September 1988 with the 15.05 service from Kyle of Lochalsh to Inverness. Note the unusual positioning of a full brake (BG) between the first and second passenger-carrying vehicles. *Les Nixon*

41

Below:

During 1986 two DMU sets were repainted in original green livery, or at least as near to it as modern safety considerations would allow. The first to receive the treatment was a Class 105 Cravens twin, Nos E53359 and E54122, and the second was a two-car Class 108 unit, Nos M54247 and M53964. The Class 108 was based initially at Carlisle and its main role was that of operating the 'Dalesman' local service over the Settle & Carlisle line. It is pictured leaving Garsdale on 9 July 1988, running as the 06.00 Skipton-Carlisle. *Jeremy Hunns*

Bottom:

The locomotive-hauled trains between Leeds and the Lancashire coast via Wennington were short-lived and soon the service reverted to DMU operation, mostly using Neville Hill's newly acquired fleet of Pacer units. On 6 August 1987 Nos 142050 and 142088 draw into Hellifield station whilst working the 17.18 Leeds-Morecambe service. Curving round to the right is the double track route to Clitheroe which remained open at the end of 1988 despite having lost its last regular traffic, a Clitheroe-Middlesbrough/Newcastle cement train, in May of that year. *Paul Shannon*

Right:

The Manchester-Bury line is worked by 1959-vintage electric units and is still signalled partly by semaphores, having escaped modernisation pending its possible conversion to a Light Rapid Transit route. Passing Queens Road signalbox on 21 May 1988 are Class 504 cars Nos M77181 and M65460, forming the 13.30 service from Bury. The rusty tracks in the left foreground lead to Cheetham Hill Junction and are used only by occasional special workings to and from the Bury line. *Paul Shannon*

Bottom right:

Having rid itself of its Class 31 duties on Trans-Pennine and Birmingham-Norwich routes in May 1988, the Provincial Sector soon had to renew its acquaintance with the type in order to provide replacement power for failed Pacers in the Manchester area. Several Manchester-Blackpool diagrams were entrusted to Class 31s with Mk 1 carriages throughout the summer timetable. On 6 August, No 31465 leaves Bolton station with the 13.32 service from Blackpool North. *Paul Shannon*

The Provincial Sector makes relatively little use of electric traction. The economics of putting up wires or laying down a conductor rail for lightly-used rural lines are such that large-scale electrification is not likely to occur in the foreseeable future. Those electrified services which exist today are of two types: local services in and around major cities; and services over lines shared with the InterCity Sector. In the former category are the suburban networks of Glasgow, Liverpool, Manchester and, to some extent, Birmingham. Only Liverpool has large sections of third-rail electrification, reaching out to Southport, Ormskirk, Kirkby, Hunt's Cross, Hooton, West Kirby and New Brighton. This network provides employment for 33 Class 507 and

43 Class 508 units, the latter having been built originally for the Southern Region and reduced from four-car to three-car formation when transferred north. Glasgow's electrified network dates back to the early 1960s but was extended substantially in the mid-1980s with the energising of Paisley-Ayr and Ardrossan/Largs branches. Here the remaining fleet of Classes 303 and 311, the original 'blue trains' which are now mostly painted in Strathclyde orange and black, is supplemented by 16 1979-built Class 314s and the latest 21-strong fleet of Class 318s. Manchester's electrified network has grown up piecemeal over the years and now covers roughly half of the suburban network around the city. Apart from the Bury line, which

uses a unique side-contact third-rail system, all routes are 25kV ac overhead, though the Altrincham and Glossop/Hadfield lines were converted in the early 1970s and early 1980s respectively from dc operation. The bulk of Manchester's ac electrified services are worked by 1960 vintage Class 304s, supplemented by 12 Class 303s from Scotland. The only units to carry the Greater Manchester livery of orange and brown are the Class 504s on the Bury line and the Class 303s. Finally the Provincial Sector operates a number of local services over the West Coast main line and its associated branches. A mixture of Class 304 and Class 310 EMUs is used on these services, which include Coventry-Birmingham, Birmingham-Walsall, Birmingham-Stafford, Stafford-Stoke-Manchester and Crewe-Liverpool.

Top:

A shortage of new Sprinter units led to the retention of four locomotive-hauled trains in each direction between Cardiff and the Northwest for some time beyond the May 1988 timetable change. Passing Chelford on 3 September 1988 is Class 37/4 No 37431 *Sir Powys/County of Powys*, hauling the 05.50 Cardiff Central-Manchester Piccadilly. *John Hillmer*

Above:

One of the more distinctive first generation DMU designs was the Birmingham RC&W 'Calder Valley' type, later designated Class 110. For many years these units were the mainstay of Manchester-Sheffield expresses as well as working the Calder Valley route. By early 1989 withdrawals had reduced the fleet to 27 power cars, all allocated to Leeds Neville Hill, and a smaller number of trailer cars shared between several depots. The 12.00 Morcambe-Leeds service is formed by Class 110 power cars Nos 52075 and 51834 and Class 108 trailer No 59246 as it approaches Settle Junction on 11 March 1989. *Paul Shannon*

Right:
Having reached the approximate halfway point on its 6hr cross-country journey, Class 156 Super Sprinter No 156440 passes through the outskirts of Nottingham at Sneinton on the 10.14 Blackpool North-Ipswich working on 1 October 1988. *Les Nixon*

Below:
Class 45/1 No 45134 heads the 10.44 Holyhead-Newcastle express past the closed Connah's Quay power station on 9 May 1987. This was the last weekday working of a Class 45 on a passenger diagram to/from North Wales. In the following week a new Sprinter service to Hull commenced operation, and the remaining locomotive-hauled trains from Newcastle were diverted to Liverpool. *Wyn Hobson*

Bottom:
With the exception of the summer-only through trains to and from London Euston, all Cambrian Coast workings are diagrammed for Derby-based Class 150/1 Sprinters. No 150111 approaches Pensarn on 20 June 1987 with the 16.37 Machynlleth-Pwllheli service. *Wyn Hobson*

Top left:
On 26 April 1988, during the second week of revenue-earning Sprinters on the Bristol-Portsmouth route, Class 155 units Nos 155324 and 155315 pass through Woolston, between Southampton and Fareham, forming the 10.10 departure from Cardiff. Electrification had been authorised for this line just six days previously. *David J. Kemp*

Left:
The remnant of the Cardiff suburban services branch to Bute Road may yet see a new lease of life, if some of the more ambitious plans for the redevelopment of Cardiff Docks come to fruition. Already the line has been diverted away from the original platform (right) to a new platform face, **being entered here by a Class 116 DMU. Some of the more moth-eaten relics from Barry Docks are now present in the museum area, shielded from BR passengers by a stout fence! The date is 8 July 1988, and the train is the 17.07 from Radyr via Cathays.** *John Glover*

Above:
The Class 33s attracted a considerable enthusiast following during their comparatively short reign on Bristol-Portsmouth workings. Running alongside one of our smaller River Avons at Limpley Stoke is Class 33 No 33003, heading the 11.14 Bristol-Portsmouth on 20 December 1986. *Ian Gould*

Top far left:
The locomotive-hauled trains on the Barnstaple branch featured a mixture of Class 31 and Class 33 power, the latter reminding the modern traveller of the line's origins as part of the Southern Railway 'Withered Arm'. On 16 May 1987 Class 31/4 No 31463 approaches Morchard Road station with the 15.48 Exeter St Davids-Barnstaple working.
Michael Mensing

Above left:
The chocolate and cream livery applied to Class 142 units 142015 to 142027 turned out to be an embarrassment for BR when the units were found to be unsuitable for working tightly curved Cornish branch lines and underwent transfer to northern parts of the system. Before its move, unit No 142022 arrives at Topsham, the only passing point on the Exmouth branch, with the 12.40 service from Exeter St Davids on 25 September 1987. *Michael Mensing*

Left:
In the shadow of Restormel Castle, near Lostwithiel, Network SouthEast liveried Class 50 No 50002 *Superb* heads west with the 07.02 Exeter-Penzance service on 30 March 1988. By this time crew training on Class 155 'Sprinters' had already started on the West of England main line, foreshadowing the virtual demise of locomotive-hauled passenger trains in the Southwest by May of the same year. *Les Nixon*

Above:
After the departure of the disgraced 'Skippers' a number of 1958 vintage Class 122 'Bubble Cars' were brought back into Cornwall to operate branch services. No longer would passengers need to cover their ears as their train squealed round the curves en route to Looe or Gunnislake! On 16 February 1988, Class 122 car No M55009 approaches St Blazey on the 08.33 Newquay-Par working, connecting at Par with the 08.28 Penzance-Paddington InterCity 125 service. *Paul Shannon*

Possibly Provincial's most heterodox service was the narrow-gauge railway from Aberystwyth to Devil's Bridge. From 1968 until the sale to the Brecon Mountain Railway it was BR's only regular steam-operated service. The terminus at Devil's Bridge is pictured on 4 June 1988, with No 9 *Prince of Wales* heading the 16.00 service to Aberystwyth. No 9, or Class 98 No 98009 as it is known by the TOPS computer, owes its origins to a GWR design of 1923. *Mike Jones*

CHAPTER THREE

Network SouthEast

When Chris Green left ScotRail in January 1986 to take up the directorship of BR's London & South East Sector, hopes were raised for a much-needed revitalisation of this dense network of services. And sure enough, it was not long before red lamp posts began to sprout at suburban stations, and rolling stock began to appear in the brash, patriotic livery of red, white and blue. As with many livery changes of recent years, public approval was mingled with scepticism and dismay when the subdued colours of blue and grey were gradually supplanted by such unashamed gaiety. But fortunately the new image was also accompanied by a determined effort to improve service quality, and a commitment in the longer term to renew much of the South East's time-worn rolling stock. Tuesday 10 June 1986 was the day everyone had been waiting for, when the new Network SouthEast identity was officially unveiled at a ceremony at Waterloo station, and shortly afterwards on 21 June nearly 200,000 people took the opportunity to sample the region's services on a £3 go-anywhere ticket.

Of the five business sectors Network SouthEast is the one with the most closely defined boundaries. It made good sense for the whole of the Southern Region to be incorporated, although the inhabitants of the Dorset town of Weymouth, 142 miles distant from Waterloo, might have been surprised to learn of their new identity! Even more bizarre, perhaps, was the inclusion of the Salisbury-Exeter line as far as Whimple, a good 163 miles away from the same

Below;
After the generally indifferent EMU designs which appeared in the 1970s and 1980s, the new Bournemouth line stock is refreshingly attractive, having wrap-round windows either side of the end gangway and an improved version of Network SouthEast livery. Internally, too, the units incorporate some innovative features, including the return to compartment accommodation for first-class passengers. A minor source of annoyance for railway enthusiasts, however, will be the lack of unit numbers on the coach ends! Class 442 stock forms the 13.30 Waterloo-Weymouth express near Nine Elms on 1 October 1988.
John S. Whiteley

Right:
Unfortunately for BR the new Bournemouth line stock was delivered late, and only five units out of the 24 on order had been commissioned by the start of the new timetable in May 1988. Finding suitable stock to operate the service in the interim was not easy, since many of the 4-REPs which had powered the previous generation of trains had had their traction motors removed for reuse in the 442s and were therefore not able to continue in service. In the event, much to the delight of enthusiasts, a number of services were handed over to pairs of Class 73/1s, with various permutations of trailer units and buffet cars providing the passenger accommodation. On 17 May, the second day of the new timetable, Nos 73136 and 73114 leave Basingstoke with an up working — note the buffet car inserted into the leading 4-TC trailer set. *Peter Tandy*

Below:
Until the arrival of the '442s', staple power for passenger trains between Bournemouth and Weymouth was the Class 33/1, which was normally coupled to the Weymouth end of one or two 4-TC units and worked in its push-pull mode. Class 33/1 No 33102 and 4-TC units Nos 8017 and 8019 approach Hamworthy station on 20 August 1987, forming the 09.32 Waterloo-Weymouth. Note the conductor rail already in place, though not yet in use. *Paul Shannon*

London terminus. Apart from the Southern Region the Network SouthEast area is bounded by Harwich, King's Lynn, Huntingdon, Bedford, Northampton, Banbury and Bedwyn. The inclusion of lines from four separate regions under a single administration was a major step for BR, breaking away from a tradition which had changed relatively little since Nationalisation in 1948.

Like those of the Provincial Sector, Network SouthEast services are not intended to be financially self-supporting. Their loading patterns are such that substantial quantities of rolling stock have to be maintained for just a few hours' use each day, trying to ferry the ever-increasing number of commuters to and from the City and other parts of central London. Nevertheless positive strides have been made towards minimising the Sector's operating loss, and over the five-year period from 1983 to 1988 the level of support from central

government was reduced by approximately one-third. This was achieved without any major cutbacks in services; on the contrary BR was confidently forging ahead with a number of ambitious investment projects, both in terms of infrastructure and rolling stock. The success of Network SouthEast in financial terms can be partly attributed to a pleasing rise in off-peak travel, helped in turn by the enormously popular One Day Capitalcard. BR's official figures recorded a rise in passenger volume of 4.5% between 1985-86 and 1986-87, and an even more impressive 7% between 1986-87 and 1987-88.

The late 1980s have seen two branch lines on the fringe of the Network SouthEast area reopen to passenger traffic: in April 1987 Corby regained its rail link with Kettering after a lapse of 22 years, and the following month saw scheduled services resume on the Oxford-Bletchley line as far as

The first of the Class 50s to come off the production line,
No 50050 *Fearless*, waits at Yeovil Junction with the 09.10
Waterloo-Exeter express on 9 May 1987.   *Ian Gould*

Bicester. Both were soon pronounced a success: at one point the Corby service was so well patronised that the conductor/guard was unable to collect all the fares during the 7¾-mile journey! The most ambitious project of all, however, was the reopening of the Snow Hill link between Farringdon and Blackfriars on 16 May 1988, allowing BR trains to run through the heart of the City between the Midland suburban line and the Southern Region network. Many passengers still use the new 'ThamesLink' trains solely as a means of reaching or fleeing from central London, especially in the peak periods, but for those who wish to cross between northern and southern suburbia without negotiating escalators and subways the new link has brought very considerable benefits. The only railway in London to have been axed completely in recent years was the link to Broad Street, which closed in June 1986 along with the one intermediate station at Dalston Junction. In many ways this was the inevitable conclusion of the reshaping of North London line services which had begun several years previously with the reopening and subsequent electrification of Dalston-Stratford. Trains from Richmond now head for Stratford and North Woolwich instead of Broad Street, whilst peak-hour services from the Watford line have been diverted over the new Graham Road curve into Liverpool Street. After Broad Street the next London terminus to succumb to the axe might well have been Marylebone, but here a rise in patronage came just in time to avert BR's closure plans and the threat was formally lifted in April 1986.

Roughly three-quarters of the 2,400 route miles covered by Network SouthEast are electrified. This includes almost the whole of the Southern Region, and also the majority of routes belonging to Anglia, Eastern and London Midland Regions. Only the Western Region relies exclusively on diesel traction for its local passenger services; here the only line likely to be electrified is the new high-speed link from Paddington to Heathrow, due to open in 1993. The vagaries of railway history have left BR with a mixture of third rail dc and overhead ac systems in the Southeast, with the former prevailing on the Southern Region together with certain North London lines. Until recently some Anglia Region lines were electrified at the non-standard voltage of 6.25kV ac, but such sections have gradually been modernised, and the standard systems now in use are 25kV ac on overhead routes and 750/850V dc on those equipped with conductor rails. Clearly the costs of installing a permanent electric power supply for lengthy sections of railway are considerable, but so too are the long-term benefits gained from electrification. Besides giving faster trains and lower rolling stock maintenance costs, electrification can sometimes be justified as a means of achieving economies of scale, particularly where small pockets of diesel traction have survived in an otherwise fully electrified area. Not all electrification schemes have involved the construction of brand-new rolling stock; in some cases the duties formerly carried out by a handful of

57

DMU sets can be covered simply by making more efficient use of an already existing fleet of EMUs.

A number of extensions have been made to the electrified network in the late 1980s. One of the biggest 'switch-ons' for many years took place at the start of the summer timetable in May 1986, when a total of four schemes were formally inaugurated. The most ambitious was the extension of third rail electrification to the '1066 Line' between Tonbridge and Hastings. The major obstacle to electrifying this line in the past had been the existence of several narrow tunnels along its length which precluded the use of standard width locomotives and rolling stock. The problem was solved in 1985-86 by reducing the affected sections of the route to single track formation. On what is now part of the Anglia Region, May 1986 saw the start of a full electrified service on three separate branches: Manningtree-Harwich, Wickford-Southminster and Romford-Upminster. The first of these formed part of the major Anglia East electrification scheme, which 12 months later brought InterCity electrics to Norwich. The other two were largely 'filling-in' schemes, which finally spelt the end of DMU-operated services on Great Eastern suburban lines and allowed Stratford depot to dispense with its allocation of DMUs. Later in 1986 the first EMUs commenced regular operation to Huntingdon, marking an interim stage of the £300 million East Coast main line electrification project. The full electrified service to Huntingdon had to wait until May 1987, by which time the wires had been extended another 17 miles northwards and Peterborough could become the new destination for outer suburban EMUs from King's Cross. Cambridge played host to its first electric trains in the early part of 1987, with the May timetable change bringing an extension of existing EMU services from Bishop's Stortford as well as electric haulage of fast trains from Liverpool Street. Electrification of Cambridge's other route to London, via Royston, was completed in May 1988, thus bringing together the wires of Great Northern and Great Eastern networks for the first time. Back on the Southern Region, the 1986 completion date of the Hastings line electrification scheme was marked by the formal commencement of another project, this time the outer suburban line from East Croydon to Oxted and East Grinstead. The new electric service to East Grinstead was duly begun in September 1987. Further west, an era came to an end in May 1988 when regular electric services were extended over the 32 miles from Branksome to Weymouth, heralding the end of the ingenious system of push-pull working which had provided Weymouth with its through London trains for the previous 20 years. Also in 1988 came the fruition of one of BR's smallest ever electrification projects: the wiring up of the 6½-mile single track branch from Watford Junction to St Albans Abbey. Authorisation to modernise the route was granted on 16 July 1987, and the new service began just under a year later, on 11 July 1988. Next in line for electrification on Network SouthEast are the

Portsmouth-Southampton and Fareham-Eastleigh lines. Conversion is already under way and is expected to be complete by May 1990. Further schemes on Southern metals will doubtless follow, for the region is now talking in terms of eliminating most or all of its remaining diesel-worked services.

The vast majority of Southern Region passenger services are worked by electric multiple-unit stock, both on suburban routes and on longer-distance journeys. The oldest stock still in common use in late 1988 was the extensive fleet of Class 415 (4-EPB and 2-EPB) units, some of which are of Southern Railway design and date back to the early 1950s. Examples may be seen in service on suburban trains on former Central and South Eastern division lines, and 2-EPBs are also used on the Richmond-Willesden-North Woolwich line. In line with BR policy for reserving new livery styles for its most modern equipment, only a few Class 415 units have so far been repainted in Network SouthEast colours, with the majority carrying standard blue and grey. Although ultimately due for replacement by a forthcoming build of 'Networker' units, some Class 415 stock has recently undergone refurbishment and will be around for a considerable time to come. Also dating back to the 1950s is a small fleet of Class 414 (2-HAP) and Class 413 (4-CAP) units; these differ from the Class 415s in having both first- and standard-class accommodation. Since May 1987 some Southern Region 'locals' have been worked by dual-voltage Class 319s, not only on the ThamesLink services for which they were designed but also on some domestic SR workings. Other suburban services to the south of London are worked by a 137-strong fleet of four-car Class 455 units, built by BREL York in 1982-87 and having a similar outward appearance to the LMR Class 317s. The Class 455 units are divided between Wimbledon and Selhurst depots and work a variety of services on former Central and South Western division lines. Apart from prototype units and the temporarily resident

Top right:

Templecombe station was reopened for an experimental period in September 1983. The reopening got off to an inauspicious start, with minimal publicity and even no mention of the new service in BR's October timetable supplement. The situation soon improved, however, and on 31 October 1987 a Class 33 locomotive, No 33112, received the name *Templecombe* in honour of the station's success. The recently smartened-up station is pictured on 8 September 1988, with Class 50 No 50002 arriving on the 09.40 Exeter-Waterloo. *John Hillmer*

Right:

One of the Southern Region's 3H diesel-electric multiple-units, No 1111, was refurbished in 1980 and given the luxuries of fluorescent lighting, gangways between coaches and public address equipment. Renumbered as Class 205/1 No 205101, this unit is seen at Uckfield on 26 September 1987, having just changed platforms before working the 11.42 service to Charing Cross. Leading into the distance is the disused formation to Lewes, a stretch of line which many would like to see reopened. *Les Nixon*

Class 508s, the Class 455s were the first Southern Region EMUs to incorporate sliding doors, a feature which is now regarded as standard for suburban units and is being extended to new builds of main line stock. The next variation of suburban EMU to appear on the SR will be a two-car variant of the Class 455, allowing BR greater flexibility with the length of its trains both during the rush hour and in off-peak periods.

For outer suburban and long-distance workings the Southern Region relies largely on a massive fleet of four-car express units with corridor connections. To the uninitiated these bear considerable resemblance to each other, and their design is similar in many ways to that of Mk 1 hauled stock. Types in service at the end of 1988 were Class 411 (4-CEP), Class 412 (4-BEP), Class 422 (4-BIG), Class 421 (4-CIG) and Class 423 (4-VEP). All the Class 411 units are allocated to Ramsgate depot and work predominantly on services to the Kent coast; they are the only SR passenger units to receive the earlier London & South East Sector livery of beige and brown ('Jaffa Cake livery') and were still being painted as such well into 1988. Of the others, Classes 412, 422 and 421 are shared between Fratton and Brighton to

Above left:

The first batch of now-generation Class 455 EMUs was outshopped from BREL York in 1982 and intended for use on suburban services radiating from Waterloo. One of this batch, Class 455/8 No 5832, calls at Datchet whilst working the 11.40 service from Windsor & Eton Riverside on 20 February 1986. It has since been repainted in Network SouthEast livery and transferred to former Central Division lines. *Paul Shannon*

Left:

Twenty-four Class 413 4-CAP units were formed in 1982 by combining pairs of Class 414 2-HAP units. Driving equipment could then be removed from the motor coaches, which were placed next to each other in the new formations. All Class 413s are used on Kent suburban services, and on 15 April 1986 units Nos 3203 and 3201 are seen passing Plumstead with the 14.36 Dartford-Charing Cross service. In the siding on the left is a rake of withdrawn 1951-type 4-EPB stock, displaced by the new build of Class 455s. *Paul Shannon*

Above:

Two vintage electric units pass Farnborough with a Basingstoke-Woking shuttle during the extravagant Basingstoke Railshow on 26 September 1987. Nearest the camera is 4-SUB No 4732, still in BR capital stock and repainted in original Southern Railway green (plus the obligatory yellow end!), and coupled to it is 2-BIL No 2090 in a similar colour scheme. *Chris Wilson*

Below:

The oldest passenger-carrying rolling stock in regular service on BR is the small fleet of electric multiple-units used on the Isle of Wight. The carriages were originally built in 1923-31 for what was then the London Electric Railway; they were converted for BR use in 1967. Looking smart and surprisingly modern in Network SouthEast livery, two Class 485 units stand in Ryde St Johns station on 27 July 1988. Trains usually pass here as well as at Sandown. Ryde works is visible on the right-hand side. *Geoff Cann*

cover a wide variety of express services, whilst the Class 423s are outer suburban units allocated (in December 1988) to Ramsgate, Brighton, Fratton, Wimbledon and Bournemouth. Also based on the Mk 1 coach design, and including some actual conversions from hauled stock, are the powered Class 432 (4-REP) and unpowered Class 438 (4-TC) units which formed the mainstay of Weymouth line trains until summer 1988. The 4-TCs have also had regular diagrams on the Salisbury line and on the Clapham Junction-Kensington Olympia shuttle. The new order on the Weymouth line is the Class 442, a totally new design from BREL workshops at York and the first Southern Region EMU type to incorporate full air conditioning as standard.

For its non-electrified routes in the late 1950s the Southern Region decided to adopt diesel-electric multiple-units in preference to the diesel-mechanical type chosen elsewhere. Many of these diesel-electric units survive today, working such lines as Ashford-Hastings, Portsmouth-Southampton-Salisbury, Portsmouth-Eastleigh, Reading-Basingstoke and the Uckfield branch. Locomotive haulage on the SR has diminished sharply in recent years, especially now that the Weymouth line has been electrified. Until the mid-1980s there were Class 33-hauled rush-hour workings on the East Grinstead and Uckfield branches, but these are now just memories. In late 1988 the Network SouthEast sector 'owned' just six out of the 17 remaining push-pull-fitted Class 33/1 locomotives, the others having been allotted to

Top:
Class 302 unit No 273 departs from Dagenham Dock station with the 14.15 Fenchurch Street-Shoeburyness service on 4 November 1988. The majority of Class 302 units still carry blue and grey livery, although those with a long-term future are being repainted in Network SouthEast colours.
Paul Shannon

Above right:
The first Class 321 EMU was unveiled at York Works on 15 September 1988. The type has many similarities internally with the dual-voltage Class 319 design, but it has a completely restyled front end and is equipped for overhead current supply only. By early 1989 Class 321 units were making regular appearances on London-Cambridge and London-Southend lines. A Shenfield-Southend driver training run passes Wickford on 16 February, formed of units Nos 321318 and 321308. *Paul Shannon*

Right:
The Anglia Region's Class 305 units date back to 1960 and still perform useful service on suburban services out of Liverpool Street. On 23 August 1988 one of the three-car variants, No 305419, shunts into the less frequently-used northern platform at Hertford East, having worked the 12.49 service from Liverpool Street. Note the unusual searchlight type signal guarding the exit from the station's main platform. *Paul Shannon*

parcels and departmental work. The Waterloo-Exeter line is the only long-distance route on the SR to enjoy locomotive haulage. Laira depot provides the resources for this service, which in late 1988 comprised 13 Class 50s and three Class 47/4s, together with a fleet of early Mk 2 coaching stock. Future haulage requirements for Waterloo-Exeter

Top:

Class 310 units Nos 310047 and 310084 depart from Roydon station with the 08.40 London Liverpool Street-Cambridge service on 26 August 1988. By this time over half of the Class 310 fleet had been transferred from the LMR to Anglia Region metals, having been replaced at Bletchley by ex-Cricklewood Class 317s. *Paul Shannon*

Above:

The second batch of 317s, Nos 317349 to 317372, was constructed at York in 1986-87 for Great Northern outer suburban services, partly as direct replacements for the Class 312s and partly with the newly electrified service to Peterborough in mind. Units 317356 and 317362 race through Welwyn Garden City on the up fast line whilst working the 09.13 from Cambridge to King's Cross on 23 August 1988. Note the short yellow band denoting the presence of first-class accommodation in one trailer of each unit — the earlier batch of 317s for the Bedford line had had their first-class sections declassified and ran as second class only until their transfer away from Cricklewood. *Paul Shannon*

Above:
Network SouthEast maintains a small pool of Class 47/4 locomotives for use on Liverpool Street-King's Lynn trains. These will be displaced by EMUs when electrification between Cambridge and King's Lynn is complete. On 24 October 1987, No 47573 *The London Standard* stands at Ely's down platform with the 10.35 Liverpool Street-King's Lynn. Beneath the level crossing lies the unusual feature of an underpass with sufficient headroom for small vehicles only; in consequence the crossing is normally used only by goods vehicles and buses. This arrangement may be found on other parts of the former Great Eastern empire, for instance at Manningtree. *John Glover*

were still under review at the end of 1988, but in the short term it was intended to replace the Class 50s with push-pull fitted Class 47/7s displaced from the Glasgow-Edinburgh line.

The suburban lines belonging to the Anglia Region bear many similarities to those of the Southern: a dense network of railways with high peak-hour loadings and a variety of rolling stock ranging from ancient to modern. The 'dinosaurs' of the Anglia Region are the four-car Class 302 units used predominantly on the former London Tilbury & Southend system, ie on services emanating from Fenchurch Street. These units date back to the late 1950s and many are earmarked for withdrawal as soon as the delivery of Class 321s allows a suitable 'cascade' to take place. Many suburban services out of Liverpool Street are worked by EMUs of a similar vintage, belonging to Classes 305, 307 and 308. The 32 four-car Class 307 units were built back in the days of 1500V dc electrification on the Great Eastern, but they were rebuilt for ac operation in 1960. The Great Eastern is also served by a 61-strong fleet of Class 315 units, built in the early 1980s to the same basic design as Classes 313, 314, 507 and 508. The most distinctive EMU type operating out of Liverpool Street is, however, perhaps the Class 309 'Essex Express' stock, built for and still operating the express services to Clacton and Walton. As with the latest Class 442 type on the Southern Region, the rounded ends of the Class 309 give this type a more attractive appearance than most of its stablemates. For semi-fast services on the Great Eastern, 19 four-car Class 312 units were built in the mid-1970s, and these were joined in the late 1980s by other Class 312s transferred from Eastern and London Midland Regions, making a grand total of 49 units. The precursor of the Class 312 was the Class 310, and

these, too, have found themselves operating in large numbers over Anglia Region metals, now that Class 317s have taken over their London Midland Region duties. For locomotive-hauled trains on the Liverpool Street-Cambridge-King's Lynn line, Network SouthEast has first refusal on three Class 47/4 diesels based at Stratford, and has also made use of the Anglia InterCity fleet of Class 86 electrics.

The Eastern Region is host to the first design of dual-voltage units on BR, the Class 313. Sixty-four of these units were built in the late 1970s for inner suburban services on the Great Northern system, working as far as Welwyn Garden City and Letchworth via Hertford North. The dual voltage capability was needed in order to operate over the former London Transport section to Moorgate, where it would be impracticable to erect an overhead power supply. The Class 312s built for the Great Northern outer suburban services have now been ousted by more modern Class 317s, partly drafted in from the London Midland Region and partly from a new build. The Class 317s work as far as Cambridge and Peterborough, with some short workings to Royston and Huntingdon.

On the London Midland Region the operations of Network SouthEast are divided into three separate sections: the Midland line to Bedford, otherwise known as the 'Bed-Pan line'; outer suburban services on the former London & North Western line from Euston to Northampton; and inner suburban services on Euston-Watford, Richmond-North Woolwich and Watford-Croxley Green lines. Of these, the Midland line has fared best in recent years: electrification and new rolling stock in the early 1980s was followed by a further influx of new stock and through services to the Southern Region before the end of the decade. St Pancras itself has been virtually abandoned by Network SouthEast, but the Bedford line now enjoys its best ever suburban service, with frequent rush-hour trains to and from Moorgate and predominantly off-peak services to Southern Region destinations such as Purley, Gatwick, Orpington, Sevenoaks and Brighton. All of these are operated by Selhurst's fleet of 60 dual-voltage Class 319s, a fleet which is set to grow even larger after the 1988 announcement of a further tranche of 20 units. Most of the Class 317s built for the Midland line are now based at Bletchley and employed on outer suburban services from Euston. In the peak hours

Above left:
The barrier line at London St Pancras has been smartened up beyond all recognition in recent years, the colourful scene being enhanced both by the Network SouthEast livery carried by unit No 317340 on a Bedford train and by the Travellers Fare sales point. This photograph is dated 7 May 1987, just one year before the inauguration of Thameslink and the consequent loss of almost all St Pancras's remaining suburban services. *John Glover*

Left:
Dual-voltage Class 319 unit No 319043 departs from St Albans City on the up fast line with the 12.37 Bedford-Three Bridges on 30 October 1988. Shortly after inauguration of the new service, commuters cynically remarked on the improbability of anyone actually wanting to travel between points such as these, but loadings have been good to the extent that a further batch of 319s was ordered during the first year of operation. An interesting feature of the photograph is the derelict St Albans South signalbox, disused since the inauguration of the St Pancras-Bedford resignalling scheme in 1981 but retained as the object of a preservation order.
Paul Shannon

Above:
After electrification of the London Bedford line in 1982 Cricklewood retained an allocation of DMUs for the Gospel Oak-Barking line. This allocation was transferred to Old Oak Common in May 1987, giving a Western Region depot responsibility for a service wholly contained within London Midland and Eastern (now Anglia) regions! Many different DMU types have been used on the Gospel Oak-Barking link, with Classes 101, 105, 116, 127, 104 and 121 all making regular appearances during the 1980s. On 3 November 1988 one of the three diagrams on the line was being worked by a pair of Class 121 single units, and these (with No 55021 nearest the camera) are pictured leaving Leytonstone High Road station on the 10.30 departure from Barking. The crossover was being used because the westbound line between Barking and Leytonstone was blocked by emergency engineering work; all freight was being diverted away from the line altogether. *Paul Shannon*

Below:
The London Midland Region's Class 501s on North London line duties were replaced in 1985 by Southern Region units of a similar vintage. One of the 'new' units, Class 416/3 2-EPB No 6328, is seen leaving Willesden Junction High Level on the 15.42 Richmond-North Woolwich service on 28 October 1987. *Paul Shannon*

Above left:

Class 313s make regular appearances on the North London line on peak-hour Watford-Liverpool Street services. In this view No 313002 arrives at Camden Road with the 08.45 'short' working from Willesden Junction (Low Level) to Liverpool Street on 4 November 1988. Although all 64 Class 313s were built for the Great Northern suburban system, their ability to operate from either third rail or overhead supply has seen them used on a variety of other routes in the 1980s, such as Euston-Watford (third rail), Colchester-Clacton/Walton (overhead) and Watford-St Albans (overhead). On the stretch of line pictured here the driver would appear to have a choice! *Paul Shannon*

Left:

The Watford Junction-St Albans Abbey electrification scheme was one of the simplest undertaken by BR in recent years, costing £675,000 for the 6½-mile single-track route. Authorisation in July 1987 was followed by inauguration a year later, giving slightly reduced journey times and a better level of comfort. Class 313 No 313005 stands at St Albans Abbey on 28 August 1988, ready to work the 17.22 train to Watford Junction. *Paul Shannon*

Above:

Since October 1987 the Chiltern lines services from Marylebone have come under Western Region control, as a prelude to the proposed sharing of 'Networker' resources with the Thames Valley line in the 1990s. The old order of first-generation DMUs and mechanical signalling is depicted at Princes Risborough on 20 August 1986, as an empty four-car Class 115 set departs for Aylesbury. In addition to the 'main' line through Princes Risborough there are still active branches to Aylesbury, Chinnor and Thame, but the impressive signalbox exterior belies the large area of empty space and the numerous white levers inside it, resulting from considerable rationalisation of the track layout in recent years. *Paul Shannon*

they are supplemented by a small number of locomotive-hauled Euston-Northampton trains, generally using Class 86 traction. The dc suburban line from Euston to Watford runs directly alongside the ac electrified West Coast main line for 16 miles and provides an interesting comparison of power supply systems. Until the mid-1980s both Euston-Watford and Richmond-North Woolwich (North London line) services were worked by a fleet of Class 501 third rail EMUs, based at Willesden. Now the North London line is worked by Southern Region units, whilst Class 313s transferred from the Great Northern system work Euston-Watford 'locals', including rush-hour-only workings to Liverpool Street. The St Albans Abbey branch is also covered by one Class 313 unit, but in overhead mode rather than third rail.

The effect of transferring the Marylebone suburban lines from London Midland Region to Western Region control in 1987 was to concentrate the majority of Network SouthEast's diesel-worked services under one administration. It is intended in the long term to cover both Marylebone and Paddington services with a single fleet of DMUs. For the moment trains out of Marylebone to Aylesbury and Banbury are formed by first-generation DMUs, mostly of Class 115. A solitary locomotive-hauled train in each direction runs via High Wycombe in the winter 1988-89 timetable, terminating and starting at Paddington instead of Marylebone. The majority of suburban services out of Paddington are also worked by DMUs, with the

Right:
The Western Region has for many years maintained a small fleet of single units for use on London area branches and also to supplement rush-hour formations on the main line. Class 121 car No 55021 calls at Castle Bar Park halt whilst working the 12.36 Greenford-Paddington on 31 October 1988. Prior to May 1988, trains from Greenford had worked only as far as Ealing Broadway. *Paul Shannon*

Below:
A clash of sectors and colour schemes at Southall on 31 October 1988, as InterCity-liveried Class 47/4 No 47501 *Craftsman* speeds towards Paddington with a rake of Network SouthEast coaching stock. The train is the 09.20 departure from Didcot to Paddington. To complicate matters further, No 47501 was actually a Parcels Sector locomotive at the time of the photograph! The once busy yard at Southall is occupied only by Class 08 shunter No 08634 and by a solitary bogie scrap wagon which had just been brought up the branch from Brentford. *Paul Shannon*

traditional fleet of Class 117s and Class 121 single units supplemented by less familiar types such as the Class 104. The Class 121 single units and their trailers are used either alone on branch line duties, eg to Greenford, or else to strengthen busy trains on the main line to Reading. Some outer suburban services in the Thames Valley still provide the opportunity to travel behind a real locomotive: in late 1988 Old Oak Common maintained a fleet of 16 Class 50s and three Class 47/4s for this work.

CHAPTER FOUR

Railfreight

The current trends of longer trains, fewer marshalling points and increased activity during the night combine to make Railfreight operations less conspicuous in the late 1980s than they were a decade or two ago. But the actual quantity of freight carried by BR in the 1987-88 financial year was 136 million tonnes, a figure not vastly different from those recorded in the mid-1970s. Remarkably, traffic levels have been kept high whilst resources such as locomotives and wagons have declined substantially in number. Like its fellow business sectors InterCity and Parcels, Railfreight is required by government to cover its costs and make a worthwhile return on its assets, and this requirement has been fulfilled in recent years as a result of successive improvements in efficiency. The management teams of the 1980s have tried to ensure a closer match between capacity and demand, so that costly resources are not used wastefully. Modern freight locomotives such as the Class 60 are designed to do the work of two or three of their smaller predecessors, thanks to their greater haulage capability and their reduced need for in-service maintenance. An availability figure approaching 100% has already been achieved by the four privately owned Class 59 locomotives: these are diagrammed for continuous operation during the

Below:
The Leicestershire coalfield may be in decline, but significant coal traffic is still forwarded by rail from disposal points at Bagworth, Coalfield Farm and Lounge, mostly for CEGB consumption at Drakelow, Rugeley and Didcot power stations. Most trains these days are in the hands of Class 58s. Here No 58047 draws its rake of HAAs under the rapid loader at Coalfield Farm on 8 July 1988: after loading it will set back into the loop (out of sight beyond the loader) and run round before departing.
Paul Shannon

working week, with just a few hours allowed for regular maintenance at the weekend. This provides a very stark contrast with most of BR's existing locomotive types and poses a real challenge for traction designers of the future. Similar strides in efficiency have been made with the wagon fleet, which comprised approximately 42,000 vehicles in 1988 and has been reduced by over 90% in the last 20 years. An increasing proportion of wagons are now privately owned, shifting the burden of maintenance away from BR and on to the customers themselves. It is now normal for wagons to be loaded or discharged within hours rather than days, and any intermediate shunting or marshalling is kept to an absolute minimum, with over 90% of freight moving direct from one private siding to another in block trains. The railway infrastructure itself has been rationalised wherever traffic levels have ceased to justify its retention: every inch of track has to earn its keep. There is no longer any need for large, sprawling marshalling yards such as those built in the 1960s. Where such yards survived into the present decade they have mostly been reduced in size (eg Carlisle, Whitemoor) or closed completely (eg Acton, Severn Tunnel Junction). The number of individual freight terminals up and down the country has been reduced, with more traffic concentrated at fewer locations and private companies being encouraged to set up distribution terminals in place of ailing railway-operated ones. The 1980s have seen a number of through freight-only lines succumb to the axe wherever an alternative (albeit longer) route could be found: casualties of this nature have included the Woodhead route, Skelton Junction-Warrington and Newark-Bottesford. Not all line closures are irreversible, however, and the Railfreight Sector has been able to justify the reopening of two lines which it had previously regarded as dispensible: Dee Marsh-Mickle Trafford on the Cheshire/Wales border and Annbank-Mauchline in southwest Scotland. The mood of the Railfreight Sector as a whole is an optimistic one, with the emphasis on revenue maximisation rather than the negative-sounding 'cost cutting' of former years: the investment schemes of today bring increased traffic and a better quality of service as well as keeping expenditure in check. Railfreight's optimism was evident at the public launch of its new identity in October 1987: the drab grey locomotive livery adopted several years earlier was supplanted

Left:

The Class 14 diesel hydraulics lasted only a few years in BR service, but many were then acquired by the National Coal Board and other industrial concerns for further use. The former No D9525, masquerading as NCB No 507, is pictured at Ashington Loop on 28 August 1986, hauling a rake of empties from Newmoor coal stacking site to Ashington pit. The Ashington rail system closed completely in March 1987, and so did the careers of the last Class 14s left in industrial service. At Ashington Loop one track still survives today, now transferred to BR ownership for the purpose of carrying Butterwell MGR trains. *Michael Rhodes*

Below:

Below:
One area where Class 37s have always felt at home is the South Wales valleys. Class 37/5 No 37691 pauses for the token exchange at Abercynon on 1 November 1988, having just brought a loaded coal train down from Merthyr Vale colliery and run round in Stormstown sidings. It will now proceed up the Aberdare branch as far as Aberaman Phurnacite plant at Abercwmboi. *Michael Mensing*

Right:
One of the busiest stretches of line for MGR workings on BR is the low-level line through Retford, which carries a steady stream of coal trains day and night from Worksop area collieries to the Trent Valley power stations at West Burton and Cottam. One such working is seen passing the delightful Manchester Sheffield & Lincolnshire Railway crossing box at Retford Thrumpton on 20 May 1988, headed by 'Red Stripe Railfreight'-liveried Class 56 No 56068.
David Moulden

by a more eye-catching colour scheme, combining three different shades of grey with red, blue, black and yellow logos for each sub-sector and individual depot badges. The new livery is not only applied to locomotives, but also to direction signs, publicity material, headed notepaper, and anywhere else where it might increase potential customers' awareness of Railfreight activities.

Over half of BR's annual freight tonnage is accounted for by coal. Most of this coal is transported direct from collieries to power stations by block merry-go-round (MGR) trains, using a system developed in the late 1960s but still unsurpassed 20 years later in its efficiency. The largest concentration of MGR services is found in and around the coal mining areas of the Midlands and Yorkshire, where 15 CEGB power stations are fed from a large number of collieries and opencast disposal points. Motive power for these trains is provided by a dedicated fleet comprising over 150 locomotives of Classes 20, 56 and 58, all based at Toton depot on the Derbyshire/Nottinghamshire border. This is a good example of the Sectorisation which characterises Railfreight operations in the late 1980s: until a few years ago the traction for these trains would have been drawn from common pools at Toton, Bescot, Tinsley and Healey Mills depots. Toton also now provides traction for MGR duties in the Northeast and Northwest. The former bring coal from northeastern pits to Blyth power station, and the latter bring coal to Fiddlers Ferry from loading points as far afield as Maryport (Cumbria) and Woolley (Yorkshire) as well as from local collieries at Bickershaw and Parkside. Separate arrangements are made for the conveyance of power station coal within Wales and Scotland. The only rail-served power station in Wales is Aberthaw, and here a fleet of Class 37/7

locomotives is maintained at Cardiff Canton to cater for all MGR services. In Scotland, MGR trains operate to Longannet and Cockenzie power stations, hauled by pairs of Class 20 and Class 26 locomotives which are maintained at Eastfield. Most MGR services on BR are timetabled with enough flexibility to allow for day-to-day fluctuations in demand, which makes detailed traffic patterns in particular areas difficult to predict. Not all MGR trains are destined for power stations: there are a number of flows to other industrial consumers, such as Bowaters (Sittingbourne), ICI (Wilton) and Castle Cement (Tring), and MGR wagons are used for import and export traffic through Hunterston, Ayr, Garston, Workington, Immingham and King's Lynn. The use of vacuum-braked wagons for coal traffic is rapidly decreasing, but flows still operating at the end of 1988 included Newport-Chinnor, Margam-Avonmouth and one or two local workings within South Wales. The market for domestic coal in Britain is a diminishing one, and the days when almost every station had its own coal yard are now gone forever. But BR has not completely abandoned domestic coal traffic, and since May 1984 what remains has been carried in modern air-braked wagons in place of the traditional vacuum-braked or unfitted vehicles. In 1986-87 a discrete Speedlink Coal Network was established for domestic coal traffic, with principal yards at Pantyffynnon, Radyr, Didcot, Washwood Heath, Toton, Healey Mills and Millerhill, and serving approximately 28 loading points and 37 discharge depots. The coal is carried in a mixture of HEA hoppers and Russell containers, and haulage throughout the network is provided by approximately 20 Class 37/0 locomotives based at Cardiff Canton. A few depots in outlying areas such as Cornwall and northern Scotland still receive

their coal by common-user Speedlink services, but these are in the minority. Household coal for Ireland is now containerised for shipment through Swansea Docks and Ellesmere Port; trains to Swansea originate at Abercwmboi, Onllwyn or Coedbach, whilst those to Ellesmere Port cover a much greater distance from either South Wales or Lynemouth (Northumberland). Also included in the Railfreight Coal sub-Sector is BR's nuclear flask traffic, which operates between Sellafield and power station railheads at Fairlie, Hartlepool, Heysham, Valley, Trawsfynydd, Berkeley, Bridgwater, Lydd, Southminster and Leiston. For this traffic a small stud of Class 31/1 locomotives is maintained at Crewe depot.

The Metals sub-Sector covers a wide range of commodities, most of them connected in some way with the production or application of steel. The raw materials for steelmaking include iron ore, limestone and scrap metal, and all of these are handled in substantial quantities by Railfreight. Imported iron ore is conveyed in block trains from Immingham to Scunthorpe, from Port Talbot to Llanwern and from Hunterston to Ravenscraig. Limestone and related products are carried, again in block trains, from Tunstead to Margam, from Redmire to Redcar, from Hardendale to Lackenby and from Thrislington and Hardendale to Ravenscraig. The principal destinations for scrap metal traffic are Aldwarke and Deepcar (Sheffield), Cardiff Tremorfa, Clydesdale and Sheerness; this traffic is ill suited to block train working because of the large number of individual forwarding points, so it is mostly carried under the auspices of Railfreight Distribution on Speedlink services. The

Above:
Despite the closure of Gateshead depot and the transfer of its Class 56 fleet to Toton, the majority of coal trains in the Northeast are still hauled by these machines, outstationed at Blyth and Sunderland (South Dock) for day-to-day servicing. Most of their duties are local, but they have a regular diagram across the Pennines to Ellesmere Port on the daily train of Cawoods coal containers from Blyth. On 19 August 1988, No 56133 *Crewe Locomotive Works* approaches Thirsk on the up slow with 6M21, the 09.55 departure from Blyth. *Paul Shannon*

Above right:
The busier of the two rail-connected pits in Lancashire is Bickershaw, where a new rapid loader was installed during the miners' strike of 1984-85. Up to six trains a day may run, all usually destined for Fiddlers Ferry power station. Class 20 locomotives Nos 20154 and 20121 are pictured at Bickershaw on 25 September 1986, prior to departure with the 7T76 local trip to Fiddlers Ferry. At the rear end of the train were two further Class 20s, Nos 20078 and 20142: it is normal practice for trains to run with two locomotives at each end from Springs Branch, since there are no longer any run-round facilities at Bickershaw. *Paul Shannon*

Right:
Healey Mills is no longer a trunk Speedlink yard, but it retains an important role in the staging of block trains and as a marshalling point for Speedlink Coal Network (SCN) services. Local 'trips' bring coal to Healey Mills from Yorkshire pits such as Grimethorpe and Kellingley, and trunk trains connect Healey Mills with other yards at Toton in the south and Millerhill and Mossend in the north. Winding out of the yard on 19 August 1988 is 6S67, the 14.52 SCN service for Gartcosh via Millerhill. The train consists of a mixture of Russells containers and HEA hopper wagons: the containers may be handled at Gartcosh, Aberdeen and Inverness, and the hopper wagons may be discharged at Haymarket, Mossend, Thornton and Dundee. The motive power is Railfreight Coal-liveried Class 37/0 No 37308, one of the dedicated SCN fleet based at Cardiff Canton depot. *Paul Shannon*

next stage in the steelmaking process is represented by coil and slab traffic between various BSC plants. The principal long-distance flows are Ravenscraig-Ebbw Vale, Ravenscraig-Shotton, Lackenby-Workington, Lackenby-Etruria, Lackenby-Corby, Port Talbot-Shotton and Llanwern-Shotton. An ingenious arrangement allows the Port Talbot-Shotton and Llanwern-Shotton traffic to be covered by the same wagons that bring Scottish coil down to Ebbw Vale, with the result that empty wagon mileage is kept to a minimum. Finished steel is the area where BR faces the stiffest competition from road transport, yet here, too, the tonnages carried by rail are substantial and increasing. A wide range of products, including tinplate, rods, bars, sections and reinforcing coils, are transported from all major manufacturing plants to a large number of destinations on BR and beyond. Much of this traffic is carried on Speedlink services, but examples of block train working are a daily train carrying tinplate from South Wales to Dover for export, and a total of five daily workings to the West Midlands, feeding local industry through the specialised steel terminals at Wolverhampton, Wednesbury, Brierley Hill and Round Oak. Semi-finished and finished steel products are carried in both directions on the Dover-Dunkerque train ferry, and there are regular import and export consignments through ports such as Hamworthy, Felixstowe, King's Lynn, Boston, Grimsby and Immingham. Traction resources for steel traffic are to some extent shared with Railfreight Distribution, since many of the flows are catered for by Speedlink services. For

Above:

A busy half-hour at Silverdale, near Stoke-on-Trent, as coal trains ancient and modern pass on adjacent tracks. On the left, Class 20 locomotives Nos 20113 and 20055 have just arrived on the single line from Madeley with a local trip from Crewe, consisting of empty vacuum-braked MDV mineral wagons. This will proceed down the branch to Holditch, where the wagons will be loaded with coal for Llanwern. On the right a rake of air-braked HAAs pass under Silverdale's rapid loader before forming a MGR service to Ironbridge power station. Silverdale closed as a passenger station when the line from Stoke was axed in 1964, but the building on the platform is still used as an office by the resident railwayman at this location. The photograph is dated 13 April 1988. *Paul Shannon*

Right:

The sole revenue-earning traffic on BR's 22-mile Wensleydale branch is limestone from Redmire to British Steel Redcar. For many years the daily train was hauled by a Class 47 locomotive, but in September 1986 Thornaby depot took delivery of two ex-Buxton Class 20s, Nos 20305 and 20306, for use on this service. Just a few weeks after their introduction, Nos 20305 and 20306 are seen passing Tees yard on 22 October 1986, with the standard rake of PGA hoppers in tow. Subsequently the locomotives were renumbered back to their original identities as 20172 and 20173, they were smartly repainted in blue with red solebars, and they were named *Wensleydale* and *Redmire* respectively. *Michael Rhodes*

trainload traffic, the Metals sub-Sector has first call on a fleet of over 100 locomotives, mostly Class 37s in their various guises, and based at Cardiff Canton, Immingham, Thornaby and Motherwell. The principal non-ferrous traffic handled by Railfreight Metals is aluminium billets from plants at Holyhead, Lynemouth and Fort William, together

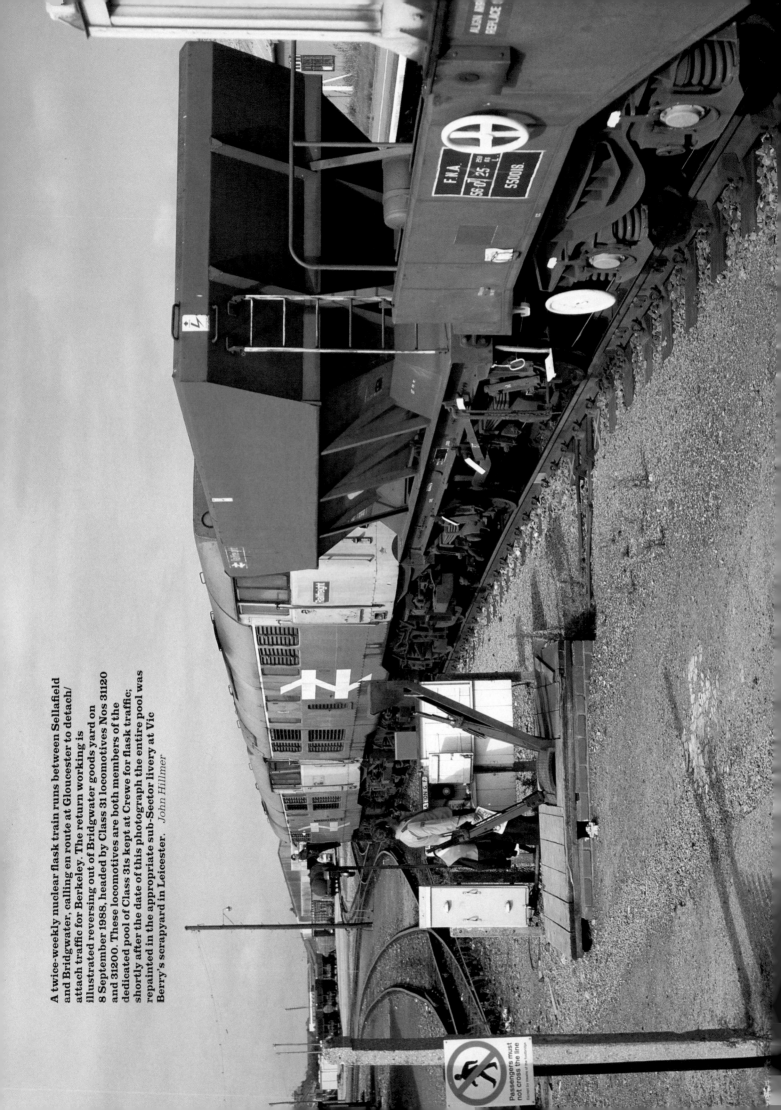

A twice-weekly nuclear flask train runs between Sellafield and Bridgwater, calling en route at Gloucester to detach/ attach traffic for Berkeley. The return working is illustrated reversing out of Bridgwater goods yard on 8 September 1988, headed by Class 31 locomotives Nos 31120 and 31200. These locomotives are both members of the dedicated pool of Class 31s kept at Crewe for flask traffic; shortly after the date of this photograph the entire pool was repainted in the appropriate sub-Sector livery at Vic Berry's scrapyard in Leicester. *John Hillmer*

with imported bauxite from Blyth to Lynemouth and Fort William. Originally included in the Metals sub-Sector was BR's Automotive traffic, although this has since been transferred to Railfreight Distribution. The term 'Automotive' covers not only finished cars and vans but also components and spares. The latter category of traffic is carried in block trains from Oxford and Swindon to Longbridge, between Dagenham and Halewood and from Germany via Dover to Wolverton; there is also some Speedlink traffic to and from Dagenham, Bridgend and Halewood. The market for finished cars and vans is very volatile, particularly where imports are concerned. Forwarding points in late 1988 included (for home-produced vehicles) Eastleigh, Dagenham, Luton, Oxford, Longbridge, Bordesley, Ellesmere Port, Halewood and Leyland, and (for imports) Dover, Southampton, Queenborough, Harwich and Immingham. Principal destinations for export traffic were Dover and Harwich, whilst domestic traffic was being offloaded at Exeter, Dagenham, Wakefield, Garston, Stranraer (for Northern Ireland), Leith and Bathgate. In addition to using scheduled Speedlink services, finished cars and vans travel on Ford company trains between Dagenham and Halewood, and there are further company trains linking Washwood Heath yard with Dover and Harwich in the south and Bathgate in the north.

Petroleum products account for just over 10 million tonnes of Railfreight traffic per annum. This figure includes a small quantity of home-produced crude oil from Furzebrook, Holybourne and Welton to Fawley and Immingham, but the vast majority of petroleum trains carry refined products such as heating oil, DERV, bitumen and aviation spirit. Rail-served refineries are located at Grangemouth, Stanlow, Port Clarence, Immingham (Lindsey and Humber), Harwich, Thames Haven (Shellhaven and Coryton), Fawley, Llandarcy, Robeston and Waterston, whilst some traffic is also forwarded from storage depots at Grain, Purfleet, Bromford Bridge (the end of a pipeline), Cardiff Docks and Bowling. Receiving depots are found in all parts of the country, some of them serving particular installations such as airports and others acting as more general distribution points. It is common practice for oil companies to buy fuel from each other in order to increase the efficiency of their transport arrangements, and it is also common for individual terminals to be served from more than one source: the Total depot at Langley, for example, was receiving scheduled trains from Humber (Conoco), Lindsey (Total), Coryton (Mobil) and Robeston (Amoco) refineries during 1988. Railfreight Distribution plays a minor role in the carriage of petroleum products where smaller quantities are involved; flows accommodated by Speedlink in 1988 included fuel oil to all BR depots, bitumen to Frome, Exeter, Elswick, Hereford and Culloden Moor, and various products to the Scottish outposts of Oban, Connel Ferry, Fort William, Corpach, Mallaig, Inverness and Lairg. The block trains which carry the majority of railborne petroleum flows are divided into several groups for operating purposes, each with a dedicated fleet of locomotives allocated to it. The first example of full-blown sectorisation within Railfreight Petroleum was the grouping together of all North Thameside workings, for which refurbished Class 37s became the standard traction type. In late 1988 there were nine Class 37/7 locomotives and one Class 37/3 allocated to this traffic, which extends west to Micheldever, east to Harwich and North Walsham, and as far north as Kilnhurst in Yorkshire. Similar treatment was given during 1988 to petroleum traffic from Stanlow, where 13 Class 47/0 locomotives were not only repainted in the latest sub-sector livery but also named after shells in honour of the company they serve. Regular destinations served from Stanlow in late 1988 were St Helens, Preston, Dalston, Jarrow, Leeds, West Bromwich, Aberystwyth and Whittington, with specials operating as required to Hereford, Newbury and Oxford. Traffic from Immingham is covered by a mixed fleet of Class 31s and Class 47s based at Immingham depot; Grangemouth traffic is covered by Class 37/0s from Eastfield; and South Wales traffic is covered by Class 37s and Class 47s based at Cardiff Canton. All petroleum traffic is carried in privately owned tank wagons, of which the commonest varieties are the 46-tonne TTA and the 102-tonne TEA. The distinctive white-liveried tanks seen in some parts of the country are used to carry liquid petroleum gas. During the 1970s and early 1980s railborne petroleum traffic was in decline, partly as a result of falling demand and partly following the construction of major pipelines to such locations as Gatwick and Birmingham. There are signs of a recovery in the late 1980s, however, with several new terminals on the drawing board and the possible introduction of new super-trains (2,200 tonnes) from Immingham to Nottingham.

One of the greatest success stories for Railfreight in the 1980s has been the conveyance of aggregates by block trains. Aggregates, or earths and stones, form the bulk of the Construction sub-Sector's business, and the annual tonnage of these materials has increased from very modest beginnings in the 1970s to a record level of 14 million tonnes in 1987-88.

Approximately three-quarters of this tonnage is destined for London and the Southeast, where demand for construction materials is high but local supplies virtually exhausted. Much of the limestone consumed in the Southeast comes from the Mendips, where the massive Foster Yeoman quarry at Merehead is complemented by the recently modernised railhead at ARC Whatley. Thirty miles away in the county of Avon is another ARC quarry at Tytherington. Between them these quarries forward over 8 million tonnes of stone by rail per annum. Foster Yeoman trains run from Merehead to 12 different discharge terminals, of which Salisbury is the closest and Harlow Mill the most distant. ARC trains serve a total of 13 terminals, ranging from Wolverton in the north to Fareham

Above left:
In matching Railfreight Metals livery, Class 37/5s Nos 37511 *Stockton Haulage* and 37521 arrive at Pengam Freightliner Terminal (FLT) with 6V67, the 23.50 from Tees Yard to Cardiff Tidal, on 3 September 1988. The main traffic conveyed on 6V67 is aluminium ingots from Lynemouth to Pengam FLT, from where they are delivered by road to Rogerstone. 6V67 is a Metals sub-Sector service which brings Thornaby Class 37s into South Wales on a regular basis. *Geoff Cann*

Left:
Up to six local trips run each weekday between Teesside and Boulby, serving the Cleveland Potash mine for which the branch was reopened in 1975. Potash and salt are carried in a variety of hopper wagons and containers, many of them redeployed from other traffic flows. On 22 June 1986 Class 20s Nos 20118 and 20137 pass Cargo Fleet with the 6P68 trip from Tees Yard to Boulby, conveying empty Procor PAA hoppers and PFA container wagons.
Michael Rhodes

Above:
Class 20 locomotives Nos 20154 and 20009 approach the site of Sealand station, on the reopened Dee Marsh-Mickle Trafford line, with the 13.11 Dee Marsh Junction-Mossend empties (6S50) on 17 October 1987. The load comprises empty BBA steel coil carriers returning to British Steel Ravenscraig. At Warrington Bank Quay the Class 20s would be removed and replaced by electric traction for the journey north on the West Coast main line. *Paul Shannon*

and Ardingly in the south. In addition, Merehead is used as a loading point for Bardon traffic to Thorney Mill, and Whatley despatches Tarmac traffic to Hayes, Mile End and Hothfield as well as Redland traffic to Woking and Sevenoaks. Most of the Foster Yeoman trains are hauled by the company's own Class 59s, whilst traction for the

ARC, Tarmac and Redland trains is drawn from Cardiff Canton's Railfreight Construction pool, which comprised 26 Class 56s, four Class 47s (including the experimental No 47901) and three Class 37/4s in late 1988. Not all the Southeast's aggregates come from the Western Region; there are also substantial flows from the Midlands, where both granite and limestone are quarried. Regular forwarding points in the Midlands are Mountsorrel, Loughborough, Cliffe Hill, Bardon Hill, Croft and Peak Forest, whilst Cauldon Low and Wirksworth have also been used on a seasonal basis for sugar stone traffic. Approximately 10 of Toton's Class 56 allocation are earmarked for aggregates traffic from the Leicestershire quarries. Away from the Southeast, limestone is moved in block trains from the Peak District to a number of sites, mostly in the Manchester area but also further afield at Washwood Heath, Leeds and Selby. The Peak District traffic is mostly covered by a dedicated fleet of 13 Class 37/5 locomotives, maintained at Tinsley but normally to be seen working in pairs from Buxton shed. Miscellaneous aggregates flows operating on BR in 1988 were Penmaenmawr-Manchester (two terminals), Rylstone-Leeds, Rylstone-Hull, Lavant-Drayton, Newhaven-Crawley, Cliffe-Salfords/Purley and Angerstein Wharf-London (four terminals). Sand traffic comprises block train flows from Middleton Towers to South Yorkshire (two terminals), from Fen Drayton to London (two terminals) and from Marks Tey to Mile End, together with Speedlink traffic from Redhill to Warrington. One noteworthy feature of the aggregates traffic as a whole is the large variety of wagon types in regular use. The majority are modern air-braked vehicles with TOPS

codes PAA, PBA (covered hoppers), PGA, PHA (open hoppers), POA, PTA or PXA (flat-bottomed opens), but this list masks the many variations of size and design which have resulted from new ideas and policies developed in the 1980s. The most exciting design is Redland's self-discharge train, which was unveiled in 1988 and has enabled deliveries to be made at several makeshift terminals, such as Cambridge, March and Stevenage. The last BR-owned vacuum-braked vehicles used in stone traffic were the HTV hoppers and MSV minerals operating from Peak Forest, but these were due to be replaced by the end of 1988. The scope of Railfreight Construction is not limited to aggregates; other commodities handled by this sub-Sector are cement, gypsum, flyash, bricks, tiles and even household

Above left:
The only freight trains to enjoy regular electric haulage on the North London line during 1988 were the Ford company trains between Dagenham and Halewood. On 4 November 1988, Class 85 No 85013 crosses from the up fast to the platform loop line at Stratford with 6M37, the 12.43 Dagenham Dock-Halewood. All car-carrying wagons used on this circuit are fitted with side shields in order to protect the load from stone-throwers and other vandals.
Paul Shannon

Left:
Almost all petroleum traffic from North Thameside is staged at Ripple Lane yard. Each day up to six trips are made between Ripple Lane and Thames Haven, using the same fleet of Class 37/7s which operate the long-distance trains. Here Class 37/7 No 37891 approaches Dagenham Dock with a loaded working from Thames Haven on 4 November 1988. *Paul Shannon*

Above:
Oil to the Highlands of Scotland is carried by Speedlink services, since the small quantities of fuel carried to individual sidings would not justify the running of a block train. The Oban branch is host to no less than three oil terminals, one at Connel Ferry and the other two at Oban itself. Class 37/4 No 37406 *The Saltire Society* crosses Loch Awe on 23 September 1988 with 7Y39, the thrice-weekly 09.45 Mossend-Oban Speedlink service. In addition to the oil traffic the train is carrying OTA timber wagons for loading at Taynuilt. *John Chalcraft*

Below:
Class 47/0 No 47125 *Tonnidae* passes along the Calder Valley line near Mirfield with 6E25, the 12.50 Stanlow-Leeds petroleum train, on 6 October 1988. No 47125 is one of the 13 Class 47s allocated to Crewe for Shell oil traffic out of Stanlow; all have been painted in Petroleum sub-Sector colours and named in Latin after shells. *John S. Whiteley*

refuse. Cement traffic is in decline at present because of changes in the industry beyond BR's control, but traffic is still forwarded in a mixture of block train loads and Speedlink consignments from production sites at Northfleet, Swanscombe, Halling, Westbury, Tring, Hope, Penyffordd, Clitheroe, Scunthorpe, Eastgate and Dunbar. Gypsum travels up the Hastings line from Mountfield to Northfleet, and flyash from CEGB power stations is conveyed to Fletton and Little Barford on the ECML. The bricks and tiles traffic has developed almost from scratch during the 1980s and currently includes Plasmor blocks from Heck to several depots in the Southeast and Redland roof tiles between a number of privately owned terminals around the country. This traffic is almost exclusively carried by Speedlink. The transporting

Top:
On 29 September 1988 the first of the Romanian Class 56s, No 56001 *Whatley*, pulls away from Frome with 6A52, the 07.40 Merehead-Thorney Mill limestone train. The formation comprises mainly 1986-built bogie PHAs owned and operated by the Bardon Group, but the first vehicle is a former Clyde Cement PBA cement clinker wagon, now with its roof removed and reclassified PHA. Formerly the Bardon trains were loaded at Frome West Yard, but this yard was closed to revenue-earning traffic in 1987 and the trains were then transferred to Merehead quarry. *Steve McMullin*

Above:
The rise in demand for aggregates in the South of England has continued unabated, and Foster Yeoman soon found itself unable to cover its haulage requirements with four Class 59 locomotives. A fifth locomotive has been introduced, but in the interim the company had to revert to using BR traction for some of its services. One working which saw regular Class 56 haulage in 1988 was the comparatively short-distance flow to Wootton Bassett, near Swindon. The appropriately named Class 56 No 56031 *Merehead* is seen approaching Fairwood Junction, Westbury, with the 6A63 11.05 empties from Wootton Bassett on 3 November 1988. The wagons used on this train are the most recent addition to Foster Yeoman's numerous and varied fleet: they are 90-tonne steel-bodied hoppers acquired on lease from Tiphook during 1988. *Michael Mensing*

Right:
Class 59 No 59003 *Yeoman Highlander* climbs out of Westbury towards Warminster on 18 July 1988 with 6O75, the 17.18 Merehead-Eastleigh working. The load of 37 4-wheel PGAs is an easy task for the Class 59 and it is able to climb the bank unaided, in contrast to the Class 56-hauled services on this route which generally need rear-end assistance. *Michael Mensing*

of containerised refuse is another fairly recent development on BR, and one that is capable of further expansion. Block refuse trains were running in late 1988 from three sites in London, three in Avon and three in Greater Manchester. Finally, the Construction sub-Sector is helping to build the railways' own future by carrying materials for the Channel Tunnel: in addition to limestone from the Mendips there are flows of minestone shale from Snowdown colliery, cement from Northfleet to Grain and tunnel lining segments from Grain to the construction site.

The Railfreight Distribution sub-Sector caters for miscellaneous flows which fall outside the scope of the other four Railfreight sub-sectors. In terms of day-to-day operations, the trains associated with Railfreight Distribution are of three types:

Speedlink, trainload and Freightliner. The Speedlink network carries smaller scale traffic flows where an entire trainload would not be justified. It is sometimes seen as the successor to the general wagonload business which fizzled out in 1984, but there are some important differences: Speedlink takes only modern air-braked wagons; Speedlink yards are small and exist for the exchange of train portions rather than for wholesale remarshalling of trains; and, last but not least, Speedlink is profitable. The first Speedlink-type service was introduced as long ago as 1973, providing an overnight link between Bristol and Glasgow. The name 'Speedlink' was officially launched in the autumn of 1978, by which time over 40 daily services were in operation. Today, the fully-fledged Speedlink network comprises nearly a

Above:

The vast majority of aggregates flows on BR are block train operations. One of the exceptions is the sand traffic from Holmethorpe, near Redhill. This travels by specified Speedlink services on a daily basis to Warrington, using a small fleet of PGA hopper wagons. The terminal at Holmethorpe is pictured on 10 July 1986 with Class 33 No 33004 in attendance. This locomotive would trip the wagons to Redhill yard, from where they would join the 6M88 Speedlink feeder service to Willesden. *Chris Wilson*

Right:

Although somewhat eclipsed by the massive output from Merehead and Whatley in the nearby Mendips, ARC's Tytherington quarry in the county of Avon is also a thriving location for Railfreight traffic. Up to five trains run each weekday from Tytherington, destined for roadstone terminals at Wolverton, Allington and Bat & Ball (Sevenoaks). Most trains are staged in both directions at Stoke Gifford sidings, adjacent to Bristol Parkway station. Edging its train forward under the loader at Tytherington on 27 July 1987 is Class 56 No 56056, a member of the Western Region Construction fleet and painted in the original Railfreight livery. After its loading has been completed the train will depart as 6C23, the 17.50 to Stoke Gifford, and the wagons will then travel forward on 6M20, the 02.20 Stoke Gifford-Wolverton. *Paul Shannon*

hundred trunk trains and a considerably larger number of feeder services, reaching virtually every corner of the system. Main yards are located at Mossend, Millerhill, Carlisle, Tyne, Tees, Warrington, Doncaster, Tinsley, Whitemoor, Bescot, Gloucester, East Usk and Willesden. The Speedlink timetable is regularly amended to take account of changing traffic patterns; this applies especially to local trip workings which sometimes serve only one or two customers. Two particular areas of growth in recent years have been home-produced timber and packaged drinks. Much of the timber traffic comes from the Scottish Highlands where it has assured the viability of a number of local freight services, whilst the drinks traffic comes largely from Western Region sources

Above left:

A unique operation on BR is the flow of gravel from Lavant, on the rump of the former Midhurst branch, to Drayton, just outside Chichester. The distance covered is only five miles, and one train makes up to four trips daily between the two terminals. The wagons are a special design of PHA bogie hopper with side discharge, and the whole train can be loaded or unloaded simultaneously. Class 73 electro-diesel No 73121 stands in Chichester goods yard on 18 August 1987 with the empty PHAs; it will proceed to Lavant when the next crew have signed on. *Paul Shannon*

Left:

Railfreight-liveried Class 56 No 56060 pulls out of Welwyn Garden City yard on 23 August 1988 after running round the 09.05 Langley Junction-Mountsorrel empties (code 6M33) in the station yard. This was a Tuesdays-only working which used the innovative self-discharge train developed by Redland Aggregates during 1988. The train must run via Welwyn Garden City because of the restricted track layout at Langley Junction. *Paul Shannon*

Above:

Class 45/1 No 45146 waits in the lower yard at Wirksworth on 29 October 1986, ready to depart with the 8P07 trip working to Derby St Marys. The train consists of short-wheelbase HKV hopper wagons loaded with limestone for use in East Anglian sugar factories. From Derby the train will proceed as 8E50, the 14.13 to Whitemoor, and then by a local service to South Lynn. In recent years the only traffic on the Wirksworth branch has been this seasonal flow of sugar stone. *Paul Shannon*

such as Park Royal (Guinness), Taunton (Taunton Cider), Hereford (Bulmers) and Truro (Newquay Steam Beer). On the debit side, the loss of Rowntrees traffic from York in early 1987 was a severe blow for Railfreight and doubtless one of the factors leading to the closure of York Dringhouses yard. For the future, Railfreight Distribution places much confidence in international traffic between Britain and mainland Europe: the capacity of the Dover-Dunkerque train ferry had already been increased with the introduction of a new vessel and terminal facilities in 1988, and the opening of the Channel Tunnel in the mid-1990s will provide an unprecedented opportunity for growth in both Speedlink and trainload traffic.

The Speedlink organisation was quick to adopt the policy of sub-sector dedication for its locomotive fleet. Tinsley was chosen as the main maintenance depot for Speedlink traction, and in late 1988 the pool allocated here comprised 102 Class 47s, 34 Class 37s and 28 Class 31s. These locomotives provide haulage for most Speedlink trains on the BR system; the main exceptions are trunk West Coast main line services, where electric haulage is the norm, and feeder services within Scotland, for which there is a locally-based pool of Class 26 and Class 37 locomotives. Railfreight Distribution's

trainload traffic is small in comparison with that carried by Speedlink, but is important enough to warrant an allocation of locomotives at Crewe, Thornaby and Plymouth Laira depots. The Crewe fleet consists mainly of eth-fitted Class 47/4s and is employed largely on chemicals and industrial minerals traffic, such as limestone from Tunstead to Oakleigh, propylene from Baglan Bay to Partington and fertiliser from Ince & Elton to various destinations. This arrangement contrasts with the one in force at Laira, where the 'trainload' Class 37/5s are employed mainly on local china clay trains but also work some Speedlink services. The inclusion of Freightliner in Railfreight Distribution dates back only to October 1988, when all BR's non-bulk freight businesses were reorganised under one administration. Prior to October 1988 Freightliner had been a separate, albeit wholly owned, subsidiary of the BRB. The logic behind the merger is simple: no longer will Speedlink and Freightliner be competing for the same traffic, and Railfreight Distribution will offer each customer

Above:

Successive changes in traction policy have seen the ICI Tunstead-Northwich trains hauled by a variety of types in recent years. After the lengthy reign of single Class 25s came pairs of Class 20s, including the Class 20/3 slow-speed variant, then pairs of Class 37s, and finally single Class 47s. Railfreight-liveried Class 47 No 47050 rounds the curve at Buxworth with 6F42, the 15.40 Tunstead-Oakleigh, on 17 August 1988. The timings on this route have been arranged so that one locomotive can make all three daily return trips, although in practice it is quite common for a change to take place during the day. *Paul Shannon*

Right:

A new limestone flow commenced operation in the Peak District in January 1988, sharing the elderly fleet of vacuum-braked hoppers used on ICI trains to Northwich. The flow is from Tunstead to Hindlow, a relatively short journey but one which involves two reversals, one at Peak Forest and the other at Buxton. In the fourth month of the new service, on 9 April 1988, Class 37/5 locomotives Nos 37679 and 37683 head south from Great Rocks Junction with 7T81, the 18.30 Tunstead-Hindlow working. The train is on the single line section between Great Rocks Junction and Buxton; the track on the left is the departure line from ICI Tunstead. *Paul Shannon*

the system which is best suited to his particular requirements. The BR Freightliner network in 1989 stretches to some 26 specialised terminals with just over 100 trains in operation each weekday. Some train services operate purely for the benefit of one major customer, such as P&O Containers, whilst others are available for more general use. Similarly the terminals served by Freightliner range from the huge installations at Stratford and Felixstowe, catering for every kind of traffic, to smaller and more specialised locations such as Swindon, where only New Zealand butter is handled. Approximately two-thirds of Freightliner business is derived from deep-sea containers, with continental and domestic traffic forming a comparatively minor element. The falling proportion of short-haul traffic was reflected in the complete closure of 10 Freightliner terminals in 1986-87, including some where substantial investment had recently been made. A happier event was the opening of Teesside's new terminal at Wilton in 1989, replacing the poorly sited facility at Stockton. One consequence of the merger between Freightliner and Speedlink will be the joint

Above:
Railfreight-liveried Class 26 No 26037 heads towards Barassie on the single line from Kilmarnock on 12 July 1988, hauling the 6R05 trip freight from Kilmarnock to Falkland yard. The train consists of three high-capacity ferry vans loaded with whisky from Johnny Walker's terminal at Kilmarnock Hill Street. These vans will be collected from Falkland yard by the passing 6E96 Stranraer-Tyne Yard Speedlink; they will be detached from 6E96 at Carlisle and join an overnight Speedlink service to Willesden; and finally another Speedlink feeder service will take them to the train ferry terminal at Dover. *Paul Shannon*

Left:
A delightful freight-only branch line remains in daily use from Markinch to the Tullis Russell paper mill at Auchmuty. The staple rail traffic to Auchmuty is china clay from Cornwall; this is delivered at the rate of one or two wagons a day by the Thornton Class 08 pilot. On 2 May 1986, No 08515 is just about to squeeze through the narrowest tunnel on British Rail (just half an inch clearance!) with a loaded TTA wagon for Auchmuty. *Michael Rhodes*

Right:
When Severn Tunnel Junction marshalling yards closed in November 1987, much of the South Wales traffic was transferred to Cardiff Tidal sidings. This is the busy scene at Tidal on 22 July 1988, as Class 37 No 37015 shunts steel-carrying wagons for 6M46, the 20.00 departure to Warrington. After completing this manoeuvre No 37015 was attached to 7M83, the 19.10 Cardiff Tidal-Bescot.
Michael Rhodes

operation of trains on certain routes, such as was tried out in the late 1970s. A new service was launched between Bristol and Coatbridge in October 1988, with a two-wagon Freightliner set conveyed once daily in each direction by scheduled Speedlink trains. Freightliner wagons are also used on several traffic flows which take them away from the established Freightliner network, such as aluminium from Lynemouth, paper from Corpach and steel from Margam. Haulage for Freightliner trains is provided from a pool of over 80 locomotives, which are progressively being repainted in Railfreight Distribution colours. The pool comprises Class 37s based at Stratford,

Above:
Tinplate is sent by Speedlink from Ebbw Vale, Trostre and Velindre to Metal Box factories at Worcester, Sutton-in-Ashfield, Aintree, Westhoughton and Wisbech. A block train also runs to Dover for continental traffic. Speedlink traffic from Ebbw Vale is conveyed by trip workings to and from Cardiff Tidal sidings, and one of these is pictured climbing the Ebbw Valley on 9 August 1988, just after passing the site of Abercarn station. The motive power is one of the South Wales Metals pool Class 37/7s, No 37711.
Michael Mensing

Class 47s based at Stratford and Crewe, and a variety of ac electric traction for use on the West Coast main line.

96

Above:

A considerable amount of Speedlink traffic is generated around Salisbury by the Ministry of Defence. At Dinton, between Salisbury and Tisbury, there are actually three separate MoD terminals in close proximity to each other. On 21 August 1987 Railfreight-liveried Class 47 No 47236 reverses out of Dinton sidings on to the single-track main line with 6L10, the 12.23 departure to Salisbury. From Salisbury the train will continue to Westbury, where connections with other Speedlink services will be made. The last vehicle in the formation is an empty TIA china clay tank en route to Quidhampton. *Paul Shannon*

Below:

Bulk china clay is railed from Cornwall to the Swiss destination of Biberist in a dedicated fleet of 23 bogie 'Polybulk' wagons. The wagons use the Dover-Dunkerque train ferry and operate a fortnightly circuit. On the outward journey the train has to be divided into two portions, running on consecutive days. One of the Dover-bound workings, consisting of 11 PIAs, is pictured joining the West of England main line at Heywood Road Junction on 17 September 1986, having just called at Westbury for a crew change. The motive power is Network SouthEast-liveried Class 50 50017 *Royal Oak*. *John Chalcraft*

Top left:
During the first full week of service for the new CDA wagons, Class 37/5 No 37675 *William Cookworthy* **arrives at Goonbarrow Junction on 16 February 1988 with empties from St Blazey. No 37675 will wait for the wagons to be loaded and then take them as far as Lostwithiel, where they will be taken down the Fowey branch by a fresh locomotive. Visible on the right-hand side of the picture are some of the old order of china clay wagons, the vacuum-braked clay hoods or OOVs, which were stored at Goonbarrow pending disposal.** *Paul Shannon*

Left·
The first of the Cornish china clay locomotives to be repainted in the new Railfreight Distribution livery was No 37673. It is seen shunting CDAs at Blackpool sidings, Burngullow, on 6 May 1988. *Hugh Ballantyne*

Above
Carlisle New Yard was opened in June 1963, with 48 up and 36 down sidings giving it the capacity to handle 5000 wagons a day. Like many other yards up and down the country, it soon became a white elephant as the quantity of wagonload traffic on BR declined, and the facilities there were gradually reduced to bring them in line with today's needs. Most Speedlink traffic in 1989 is handled in the 12 remaining up departure roads. Leaving the yard on 15 July 1988 is Class 85 No 85021, heading 6V92, the 16.10 Mossend-Gloucester Speedlink. The first wagon in the train is a PBA china clay carrier, returning empty from Mossend to Cornwall. *Paul Shannon*

Above:

A daily block train connects the Spillers terminal at Wisbech with the Deanside Transit distribution depot near Glasgow, for the conveyance of a wide variety of food products. The train is pictured during loading at Wisbech on 7 September 1987, with Class 47 No 47236 already coupled up and ready for departure. The northbound working runs as 9S93 (35mph) to Whitemoor and 6S93 (60mph) from Whitemoor to Deanside. *Michael Rhodes*

Below:

Painted in the short-lived 'Red Stripe Railfreight' livery, Class 47 No 47157 arrives at Temple Mills yard with 6C84, the 16.10 'local trip' from Bow Goods. The train consists of empty TTA carbon dioxide tanks for Avonmouth, empty coal hoppers for South Wales, and empty OBA/OCA open wagons for the Plasmor terminal at Heck (Yorkshire). All these vehicles had been unloaded at Bow. After arrival at

Temple Mills No 47157 would couple up to 7M82, the evening Speedlink working to Willesden. Overhead electrification was extended to Temple Mills in early 1988 as part of the North London line scheme, but diesel haulage remained the norm until at least the end of 1988. *Paul Shannon*

Right:

The branch to Seaforth Container Terminal in Liverpool Docks is traversed by a daily Freightliner working to and from Garston or Crewe, where connections with trunk services are made. On 2 April 1986, Class 47 No 47380 ambles along the branch with 4F67, the 17.40 Seaforth-Garston. An unusual feature of this branch is the Allied Mills grain 'terminal': this actually consists of a discharge hopper situated directly above the 'main' running line to Seaforth Container Terminal, and thus can only be used at times when no Freightliner train is due! *Paul Shannon*

Above:
A new sub-class was born during 1988, the Class 86/5. Intended for heavy freight work and fitted with TDM multiple working equipment, the first few locomotives were making regular appearances by the end of the year on a range of Speedlink and Freightliner services. No 86502 carries the latest Railfreight livery and 'general' red and yellow logo, since it is not allocated to any one particular sub-Sector. It is pictured heading south on the West Coast main line near Swynnerton on 29 October 1988 with 4L76, the 13.16 SO Trafford Park-Tilbury Freightliner train. This service will call at Rugby on its way south in order to collect a portion from Leeds.   *Paul Shannon*

Below:
Felixstowe North Freightliner Terminal on the evening of 13 June 1988, showing Class 37 locomotives Nos 37004 and 37055 waiting to leave with the 19.30 departure to Stratford. This train will use the direct link to Trimley which was opened in March 1987 to provide easier access to and from Felixstowe North.   *Michael J. Collins*

CHAPTER FIVE

Parcels and Departmental

Whether measured by its annual turnover, by the spread of its operations or by its resources, the smallest of BR's business sectors is the Parcels Sector. It also has the lowest profile in the eyes of enthusiasts and other followers of the railway scene, partly because most of its activities are concentrated during the hours of darkness. Parcels remain an important source of traffic on BR, however, and despite a small operating deficit in the 1987-88 financial year this sector is generally self-supporting and free from government subsidy.

Recent years have seen British Rail withdraw completely from two areas of operation: Collection & Delivery, and Newspapers. The collection & delivery business was highly labour-intensive and notoriously inefficient, and was abandoned in 1981. The newspapers business survived relatively intact until the late 1980s, but the loss of News International traffic in 1986 and Mirror Group traffic in 1987 left many trains half empty and soon led to the distribution network as a whole becoming unviable. The result was that, on 10 July 1988, BR stopped running newspaper trains altogether, and transferred any residual traffic (mainly periodicals

and a few 'dailies' such as the *Financial Times*) to scheduled passenger trains. Most of the hundred or so daily newspaper trains had run from either London or Manchester to various destinations in the south and north of the country respectively. From Paddington, for example, regular destinations were High Wycombe, Aylesbury, Banbury, Slough, Reading, Oxford, Bristol, Newton Abbot, Penzance, Gloucester, Worcester, Swansea and Milford Haven. Departure times were spread through the early hours of the morning, and the empty coaching stock returned to carriage depots later in the morning or afternoon. The

Below:
Class 45/1 'Peak' No 45126 approaches Manchester Victoria with the Sunday Leeds-Red Bank newspaper empties on 15 February 1987. Upon arrival at Victoria No 45126 will run round its stock and then take the line to Red Bank, visible on the left-hand side of the picture. The Leeds-Red Bank train was a favourite for 'Peak' haulage during 1987, although Class 47s and Class 31s were also used during the last months of the train's operation. The rolling stock consists mainly of four-wheel NPVs, the last of which were withdrawn in 1988. *John S. Whiteley*

Above:
Class 37/0 No 37027 *Loch Awe* approaches Culloden with the Perth-Inverness vans on 27 June 1986. In the following month this locomotive was renumbered 37320 and renamed *Shapfell* before joining the dedicated Hunterston-Ravenscraig pool. No 37027's old nameplates were transferred to ETH-fitted loco No 37409. *John Chalcraft*

Right:
Leaving Crewe on Saturday 28 May 1988 is 4D02, the 09.25 parcels working to Chester. The stock comprises one of the original Class 128 parcels cars, No 55993, and a two-car Class 114 conversion, Nos 54902 and 55932. Also tacked on to the end of the train is a two-car passenger DMU on its way from Shrewsbury to Chester DMU depot. The working pictured here was withdrawn from the timetable in October 1988. *David Rapson*

Left:

A number of Class 114 'Derby Heavyweight' DMUs were converted for parcels use in the late 1980s, as part of the Parcels Sector's plans to reduce its commitment to locomotive-hauled trains and thereby considerably reduce its costs. Cars Nos 54900 and 55930 pass Middleton Junction signalbox on 16 August 1988, running as 4M27, the 14.46 Leeds-Liverpool Lime Street. Their former identities were Nos 54034 and 53010 respectively. On the extreme right is the disused branch to Chadderton coal depot.
Paul Shannon

empties were, of course, better known amongst enthusiasts than the loaded workings; some trains such as the Sunday afternoon Heaton (Newcastle)-Red Bank (Manchester) vans will be sadly missed.

Most Parcels Sector business in 1989 falls into one of two categories: it is either BR's own Red Star traffic, or else it is Royal Mail traffic. The essence of Red Star is same day (or overnight) delivery, and this is achieved by making extensive use of timetabled passenger trains which are both faster and more frequent than traditional parcels trains. Approximately 500 passenger stations act as loading and unloading points for Red Star traffic. The Post Office also sends much of its mail and parcels traffic on passenger trains, as well as using the network of dedicated parcels services. The latter have declined in number during the 1980s, with certain destinations such as Stranraer now served by a road connection rather than by a direct rail service, but the network has seen some additions,

too, such as the Gillingham-Preston working which started in 1987. One area of operations which remains buoyant is the network of overnight Travelling Post Office (TPO) trains, where mail is sorted on the move. This is an area where the railway has an intrinsic advantage over its main competitors, the road hauliers. The detail of the TPO network has undergone a number of changes in the last couple of years, all ultimately in an effort to improve the speed and reliability of household letter deliveries. Approximately 35 TPO trains run each night, many of them on trunk passenger routes such as London-Swansea, London-Glasgow and Plymouth-Derby, but also including some less likely journeys such as Whitehaven-Huddersfield and Cardiff-Shrewsbury-York. One surprising feature of the TPO network is the virtual absence of such trains on the East Coast main line, in similar vein to the lack of overnight passenger services on this route.

The Parcels Sector uses Class 85 or Class 86 locomotives to haul its trains on the West Coast main line, and is also responsible for a fleet of approximately 90 diesel locomotives for use on non-electrified lines. In late 1988 the sector 'owned' 28 Class 31/4s based at Crewe, seven Class 33/1s based at Eastleigh, and 56 Class 47/4s based mainly at Bristol Bath Road and Stratford. Most of these locomotives carried either standard rail blue or InterCity livery, making their sector allocation difficult to discern from the lineside. The rolling stock used on locomotive-hauled parcels trains

consists entirely of bogie vehicles suitable for high-speed running. The fleet has shrunk from a huge and varied one to a small, standardised one in little more than a decade. Whilst parcels vans from all four pre-Nationalisation companies survived into the late 1970s, these have now all been withdrawn in favour of three BR standard designs. The types which survive are the BG gangwayed brake van (TOPS codes NBV, NCV, NCX, NDV, NDX, NEA, NEX, NHA), the non-gangwayed GUV van (TOPS codes NJV, NJX, NKV, NLX, NMV, NXA, NXX), and Travelling Post Office vehicles (TOPS codes NSV, NSX, NTX, NUV). The fleet also includes a number of NNV and NNX courier vehicles which were converted from Mk 1 passenger stock in the late 1980s. As shown by the range of TOPS codes for each type, there are a number of detail variations between batches, many of them the results of subsequent modifications such as air braking, electric train heating and 110mph capability. The type used most extensively on passenger trains is the BG, which on West Coast main line trains is often the only carriage with a guard's compartment and therefore a necessary element regardless of parcels traffic. GUV vans may be attached to passenger trains where the volume of parcels traffic is large, such as London-Holyhead.

Consistently with the general move away from locomotive-hauled trains on BR, the Parcels Sector has greatly enlarged its fleet of diesel parcel units (DPUs) in the late 1980s. This policy has enabled the sector to reduce its costs considerably. The only purpose-built DPUs are the five surviving Class 128 single units, maintained at Cambridge. These date back to the late 1950s but are still performing useful service and have now received that most striking livery of the 1980s, Post Office red. The majority of the DPU fleet is made up of conversions from passenger stock, with five different types in use by the end of 1988. The most numerous fleet was formed in the mid-1980s by the conversion of Class 127 DMUs displaced from the St Pancras-Bedford line; 21 such vehicles were on BR's books in late 1988, all adapted for parcels use by the removal of seats and the fitting of roller shutter doors. The

Below:
For some time after Network SouthEast's adoption of red, white and blue as standard garb for its rolling stock, Southern Region workshops at Selhurst and Eastleigh continued to adorn Kent Coast Class 411 units in the earlier 'Jaffa Cake' livery of orange and brown. Also so treated were the 1959-built Class 419 motor luggage vans. On 4 September 1987 a Dover-Victoria boat train passes Shakespeare Cliff with Class 419 luggage van No 9005 at the front and two Class 411 4-CEP units providing the passenger accommodation. *Michael J. Collins*

Right:
The 10.39 Southampton-Clapham Junction empty van train heads east near Basingstoke on 23 April 1987, hauled by Class 33/1 No 33112 and Class 33/0 No 33047. The former locomotive was on test from Eastleigh where it had just received an intermediate overhaul. *Colin J. Marsden*

Below right:
Class 33 No 33006 reverses empty TPOs from St Philips Marsh into Malago Vale carriage sidings on 5 May 1988. The stock would later form the 19.42 postal to Newcastle. Malago Vale sidings closed during the summer, and Class 33s were to become a rarity in the Bristol area shortly after this photograph was taken. *Geoff Cann*

Above:
During 1988 three Class 31/4 locomotives were named after preserved railways. No 31413 received its name *Severn Valley Railway* at Bewdley, and was also repainted in a unique combination of rail blue, light blue, yellow and red. In some quarters the locomotive came to be known as 'Ice Cream Van No 2', following the example set by Class 25 No 25912 (now withdrawn). Like many Class 31/4s, No 31413 is allotted to departmental work, and on 18 May 1988 it is seen departing from Penmaenmawr with 7K11, the 10.11 ballast working to Chester. *Don Gatehouse*

remainder of the DPU fleet in late 1988 comprised 15 Class 114 vehicles (seven two-car units and one spare car), four two-car Class 101 units, three two-car Class 105 units, and one two-car Class 116 unit. The Class 127s are all allocated to Longsight depot, whilst most of the others are maintained at Cambridge. One Class 114 unit had been repainted in Post Office red livery by the end of 1988, with the others carrying either standard rail blue or blue with red stripe (Red Star livery). The use of electric multiple-units in dedicated parcels traffic is more restricted, with just three Class 308 conversions allocated to Ilford and 10 Class 419 Motor Luggage Vans based at Ramsgate. For many years the Class 419s were used mainly on boat trains between London and the Channel ports, but by late 1988 more examples were beginning to run singly and some had received Post Office red livery.

Also illustrated in this final chapter are a cross-section of departmental workings on BR. Departmental workings are those which carry no revenue-earning traffic and are funded by the relevant engineering or research department. Most materials for consumption by the railway itself fall within the departmental category, with the notable exception of traction fuel oil which is now classed as revenue-earning traffic. Approximately 280 main line locomotives are allotted to departmental work, including examples of Classes 20, 26, 31, 33, 37, 47, 50 and 73. They are scattered widely between maintenance depots in all corners of the system and, in theory at least, are more likely to stay near to their home base than the average Railfreight locomotive. Many departmental trains are not timetabled and run purely according to local needs, ranging from weekend track maintenance to unplanned assistance with derailments and other emergencies. Those that do appear in the timetable include a large number of ballast trains from quarries or loading points such as Meldon, Merehead, Machen, Bayston Hill, Hartshill, Cliffe Hill, Croft, Mountsorrel, Penmaenmawr, Hexham, Hillhouse and Inverkeithing. Some quarries supply railway ballast for a large area of the network: much of the Southern Region is served from Meldon, for example, and Penmaenmawr despatches trains to destinations as far north as Bamber Bridge and Carnforth. During the 1980s BR has made efforts to reduce the number of separate quarries forwarding ballast traffic, sometimes resulting in the closure of a railhead as has occurred at Ribblehead and Blodwell. Other scheduled departmental services include those carrying engineers' materials such as spoil, and those conveying revenue-earning wagons or coaching stock to and from repair works.

Top left:
Penzance station on 4 May 1988, with two 'Hoovers' awaiting their respective departure times. On the left is No 50030 *Repulse* with the 19.22 'Great Western Postal' for Paddington, and on the right is green locomotive No 50007 *Sir Edward Elgar* with the 18.30 local to Plymouth.
Hugh Ballantyne

Left:
One of the last Class 27s in revenue-earning service, No 27059 shunts a rake of ballast hoppers in Burntisland yard on 12 April 1987, having spent much of the day on tracklaying duties north of the station. Upon withdrawal No 27059 was happily not consigned to the cutter's torch but was purchased by Sandwell Council for display at the Birmingham Railway Museum at Tyseley. *Les Nixon*

Top left:

Class 85 No 85007 heads south on the West Coast main line near Whitmore with a trainload of concrete sleepers on 29 October 1988. The working is the previous day's 12.15 Newton Heath-Fratton special, reporting number 7Z40. Many departmental wagons are cast-offs from the revenue-earning fleet, and the vehicles which form the bulk of this train are no exception, having begun their existence as STV tube wagons. *Paul Shannon*

Centre left:

Two Class 03 shunters have found a home on the Isle of Wight, Nos 03079 and 03179. Both are allocated to the Departmental Sector and at the time of writing are stationed at Sandown and Ryde respectively. No 03079 is pictured on 25 February 1987 standing alongside Sandown's bay platform, from where connecting services to Merstone and Newport once departed. *Hugh Ballantyne*

Bottom:

When Derby RTC locomotive No 97203 (formerly No 31298) was severely damaged by fire in April 1987, a replacement was quickly found in sister locomotive No 31326. This was duly renumbered 97204 and eventually repainted in a slightly revised version of the RTC's striking livery. On 21 July 1988 No 97204 is pictured at the site of the closed Etwall station with vehicles RDB975046, Lab Coach 11, RDB999900 and auto-trailer RDB975076 in tow. *Hugh Ballantyne*

Right:

Most of BR's departmental vehicles are acquired second-hand from capital stock, but during 1987 a brand-new track recording unit was constructed for Derby Railway Technical Centre, based closely on the Class 150/1 'Sprinter' design. The new unit is classified Class 180/1 but carries only individual coach numbers DB966000 and DB966001. It is pictured on Horfield Bank on 13 June 1988. *Michael Mensing*

Below right:

Railfreight Class 31 No 31276 passes Stratford on 9 July 1987 with recently overhauled Class 312/0 unit No 312719 in tow. The 26 units of this sub-class were built for Great Northern outer-suburban services, but were gradually transferred to Great Eastern lines as Class 317s from the St Pancras-Bedford line became available as replacements for the Great Northern's Class 312s. No 312719 was one of a small batch transferred to the Great Eastern as early as September 1986. *Paul Shannon*

Sunset over Manchester's Red Bank carriage sidings on 9 January 1988, with a mixture of passenger and parcels stock present. *Les Nixon*